THE
Third
THIRD

THE *Third* THIRD

Seeing the World Through Rose-Colored Bifocals

Claire Mitchel
Based on her column in The Miami Herald

Bartleby Press
Silver Spring, Maryland

Printed in the United States of America.

Published and Distributed by:

Bartleby Press
11141 Georgia Avenue
Silver Spring, Maryland 20902

Library of Congress Cataloging-in-Publication Data

Mitchel, Claire, 1921–
   The third third : seeing the world through rose-colored bifocals / Claire Mitchel.
     p.   cm.
   Based on the author's column in the Miami Herald.
   ISBN 0-910155-17-8
   1. Mitchel, Claire, 1921– . 2. Aged—United States—Biography.
3. Old age—United States. I. Title.
HQ1064.U5M58 1991
305.26 ' 092—dc20   90-19246
                                           CIP

To my almost always patient husband, Arnie.

Contents

♦

The Way We Are **95**
A Good Marriage Is Not A Product; It's A Process *97* ◆ First Third
Logic *100* ◆ Spending Habits Steeped In Memories Of '30s *103* ◆
Doctors' Ills Kill Faith Of Patients *106* ◆ Harry's Retirement Haven *109*
◆ The Best Surprise Is No Surprise *112* ◆ Widowed Loners Need Not
Be Lonely *115* ◆ Sweet Righteous Indignation *118*

It's Not So Easy **121**
Fair Weather Friends *123* ◆ Driver's Responsibility—Knowing When
To Stop *126* ◆ Too Much Of A Good Thing *129* ◆ Biopsy Offers
Reprieve *132* ◆ Exercise: Painful Precaution Against Aging *135* ◆
Healthy Life Mends A Tattered Heart *138* ◆ An Insightful Event *141*
◆ Whip Those Flabby Brains Into Shape *144*

Yesterday Visits Often **147**
Mayme Made Her Mark *149* ◆ Daughter's Birthday: Memories Of Pain
And Pleasure *152* ◆ Just For The Record *155* ◆ My People In
Pictures *158* ◆ A Reunion With Youth *161* ◆ Colorful Characters In
Family Picture *164*

Wisdom Sustains **167**
Mother's Myths, Father's Fables *169* ◆ Lessons From The Laureate *172*
◆ We've Seen It All, But We're Not 'Know-It-Alls' *175* ◆ Comfort's Cost
Is Loss Of Freedom *178* ◆ Proud Parents Pave Path *181* ◆ Eleanor: The
Lady Was A Legend *184* ◆ Old Age Just A Stage Of Life *187* ◆ Money
Talks—Can We Hear? *190* ◆ You Can't Buy Happiness, But Americans
Sure Do Try *193* ◆ Good Grief *196*

After Today **199**
Now's The Time To Sit Back And Savor Life *201* ◆ Aging Children
Anguish As Parents Linger *204* ◆ The Hurting Spot *207* ◆ Today Is
The Rainy Day *210* ◆ When Kids Grow Up, The Silence Is
Deafening *213*

We're Off Our Rockers **217**
Call Me Old And Fading, But Don't Call Me Out *219* ◆ Dare To
Dream *222* ◆ The Young Live Like There's No Tomorrow *225* ◆ Fruit
Of Age Is A Free Spirit *228* ◆ Passion Is Revived By A Well-Built
Model *231* ◆ Home Sweep Home *234* ◆ Love And Acceptance *237* ◆
We've Earned Our Aches, Pains And Foibles *240*

Preface

♦

From early childhood my mother taught me to clean up after myself, to "be cooperative" (the role of most females of my generation), and to celebrate life. My father, who lived to 98, preached that life is fragile: "Make the most of each day, and use your eyes to perceive what you want," he would say.

Both had come from Poland in their early teens and struggled in the lot of immigrants. They taught me to deal swiftly with adversity and to point myself in the direction of a party.

When illness struck, or during the Depression, we would think of a good reason for a party. Sometimes it was simply to celebrate Tuesday.

"You don't need a reason or other people," said Mother. "All you need is a pot of coffee." And Papa would add, "Bring a clean pair of eyeglasses to help you see things brightly."

When *The Miami Herald* invited me, at 64, to write a column, the 34-year-old editor hesitated. "Can you dust off the journalist's five W's—the who, what, when, where, and why?" he asked. "Can you apply that to the people who live in condos, the retirees, those who are slowing down?"

My response was to take the assignment to write a weekly column with my own set of five W's: "What's Wrong With Women's Wrinkles?"

We decided to call it The Third Third to include all those over 60. That was 1985 and now, more than 270 columns later, the concept has taken on its own persona.

The Third Third has been adapted for the theater by Vinnette Carroll of Emmy and Tony fame, who mounted thirteen columns, some to music, titled "At Our Age We Don't Buy Green Bananas."

Senior InNOVAtions Seminars are a monthly series at Nova University dealing with issues of aging based on readers' response to "The Third Third" columns. This past year I appeared 39 times on a local CBS television affiliate with commentaries about The Third Third. Magazines and newspapers elsewhere have picked up the concept.

The mail has become a means of dialogue with readers, including a surprising number of young people. I respond either in the paper or by letter. The *Miami Herald* Speakers' Bureau sends me to many clubs and organizations to provide "eyeball-to-eyeball" contact with the people about whom I write. They help me with the "how to" of living well these later years, from a broad perspective.

They have also shown me that we can anticipate at least twenty additional years beyond those any previous generation could dream about. With our reproductive role fulfilled, today is our day to relax, securely and serenely. With lessened responsibilities, we have the freedom to choose from many options.

We are a phenomenon, the first group in history that has a life after work. We are active, alert, healthy, and self-sufficient. We live a long time, longer than many planned. The choice of how to fill these bonus years is ours. They can be the best of all.

We're off our rockers. We don't want to sit listening to our arteries harden. Today is not tomorrow.

What role we select at this time of life, barring disease, from the cornucopia of choices is our own decision. What is the place for senior citizens, retirees, golden-agers, any of the euphemistic names we call ourselves? What can we give to life and what do we expect of life at this age?

We who are over 60 today are a new generation. We have no paths to follow; no role models. We can design our own future. We don't have to live by the old decrees that damn the elderly. We can make our own new rules of self-acceptance and self-actualization; not with acquisitions or with tummy tucks, but with self-satisfaction for our accomplishments and potentials.

We are a new breed—not the grey, sad, dreary elderly of myths. We were toughened by the Depression and wars we have lived through, and strengthened by the many changes we encountered in this century.

We have done all the woulds, coulds, and shoulds. Now is our time to rest on our laurels, to savor life's rich rewards. This is our time off for good behavior.

We await our new place in society and the new challenge that will bring. It is to the advantage of the young to develop with us a modus vivendi so our country can begin to move from the youth culture to accept the changed image of growing older, and to look forward to this age.

But we are realistic enough now, when we are clear of mind, to know not all of us will be lucky to live until we die; some of us will fade away more slowly, suffering a long goodbye, like the last dry leaf in fall. Some of us will become a burden to our children and to our community.

We will have new community and national needs for

adequate health care, housing, transportation, job training and re-training, among other vital services. Despite those needs we want to live independently until the day we can't.

We of the Third Third, who are able-bodied and of good cheer, can view the world through rose-colored bifocals, sending the message that living longer can be a time of optimism, enthusiasm and humor. We have the opportunity and the obligation to live life to its fullest; to keep dancing until the party's over.

To have reached this age, in which we can choose our lifestyle, and can be aware of the opportunities for expanding, is to live to the end with self-esteem, our greatest possible achievement. This self-esteem will bring respect for aging.

This is the dessert time; time for sweet relaxation. Join the celebration of having come this far.

I trust this book will say something of significance to my generation and to those who follow. I consider it a privilege to be an observer and reporter for the Third Third, and to document the process as we age. The weekly self-examination in writing the columns has brought me strength and comfort. I hope the book will make a difference to the reader as well.

C. M.
November, 1990

Acknowledgements

♦

I n my seventieth year there is an accumulation of people who have affected me, my thinking, my writing, and thus, this book. What and who left the deepest imprint and offered the most helpful hand in leading me here is impossible to say.

My parents and children, of course, are the closest. They have the most affect on who I started out as and on who I became. My husband Arnie, with whom I've spent the last 50 years, is my best friend and severest critic.

Seymour and Marion Furman are family who, no matter what I say, write, or do, are ever devoted.

Ron Ishoy, my erstwhile mentor, hired me at *The Miami Herald* and encouraged me to say things that were new, all the time teasing about newspaper people writing "instant literature." Amy Brunjes, Chris Mobley, Carol Weber and all the youngsters at the newspaper with whom I quarrel about the vernacular of my generation, but who abide me nonetheless.

Joyce Guterman is my loyal listener and friend. Esther

Powitt helps at my side even when I'm not sure of what I want. Fonda Kramer, my sporting friend, helps me keep my body agile. Gert Cartino, Patricia Gershwin and Ruth Spaet, friends beyond the call, fastidiously read and helped select these columns to be included herein. Also, thanks go out to the many friends and acquaintances who lead me to stories.

Jeremy Kay, my publisher, recognized and chanced a new direction. The readers and editors of the newspapers in which the columns are syndicated seem to have found a kindred voice.

Vinnette Carroll made the printed word come to life. Dr. Stephen Goldstein gave me the lecture podium, and Donn R. Colee, Jr. gave me TV visibility.

I'm indebted to the many devoted people in The Third Third who write to me, attend the lectures and seminars, and who give me the benefit of their views on this time of life. Mostly my thanks go to the friends and acquaintances who are the subject of my essays, who shared their lives with me. They, too, believed that they are interesting but not unique, and that their particular story will become the general.

With All Our Heart

The S.O.B.

◆

Through the din and stir of the large condo theater, we looked for the friends who had asked us to join them. Searching the crowd, I heard a piercing shriek as someone called my name. I turned toward the caller, and saw a face from the distant past. I'll call her Marion.

I hadn't seen her in 30 years since I left the small New Jersey town in which we had lived as young marrieds. The years showed on her so that at first, I did not recognize her.

Sooner or later in South Florida, you run into everyone you've known; therein lies the pay-off for a moral past.

The performance was about to start. In charade-like gestures, I offered to meet her later.

As the curtain opened before us, my mind wandered back to the days when we were neighbors, in the first years after our husbands returned from World War II.

My faded memories were of Marion constantly being harried. She'd lose her keys, or leave her wash out on a rainy day. Each of her children presented a challenge she

3

couldn't cope with. All of her vexations were due, she would say, "to my Frank, that S.O.B."

She always complained she was short of money; "My Frank, the S.O.B." constantly lost money at poker games. She found a reason to knock on my door at least twice a week. Confined to quarters by housework and young children, I welcomed her need for a confidante.

"Do you know what time my Frank, the S.O.B., came in Tuesday night?" she would ask. It was difficult not to know. Sometime past midnight, we would hear a car door slam. Minutes later we would hear muffled sounds of voices that soon grew to battle pitch. Their quarrels — and who didn't scrap in those struggling times — were so routine that we neighbors paid little heed.

I moved later to another part of town, and would see Marion once in a while at the grocery store or PTA meeting. Each time we met, shortly after the opening niceties, she would fill me in on her latest distress.

"You can appreciate the situation," she would say. "He tells me to take a kid to the dentist without paying the bills. That's my Frank, the S.O.B."

A few times I hesitatingly suggested that she try life without him. It would be twice as hard alone, she would answer, and even if he was never home when he was needed, the children shouldn't grow up without a father in the house. No, she would continue to suffer in silent martyrdom.

I moved to Ohio in 1955 and didn't see Marion again until our encounter in the theater. During intermission, I wended my way over to her and her four women friends, and was introduced as her former bosom buddy. Meeting in Florida makes anyone from the past a link with the familiar — an ally. I couldn't resist asking, "How's your Frank?"

"Oh," she replied sadly, lowering her eyes. "I guess you didn't know. My Frank passed away four years ago. That's when I moved to Florida."

She turned to her companions and triumphantly said, "She knew my Frank. She can tell you about him." This seemed to be a request for testimony on Frank's virtues, which I hesitated to give. So I just smiled. We chatted until the flickering lights summoned us to the next act.

When the final curtain closed, I made sure to catch Marion's eye and took her aside so we could reminisce in private.

"I'm so pleased for you that your Frank mended his ways and became such a model of a good husband later in life," I said.

"Oh, no," she said. "He was the same Frank, the S.O.B., until the day he died."

With a twinkle in her eye, pointing her thumb toward her heart, she added, "But he was MY S.O.B."

Second Time Around

♦

I t was good to see Florrie across the room but I couldn't
be sure that the brightly dressed woman was the work
colleague I hadn't seen for six years. The last time we
talked she was in the throes of divorce. Then she looked
drab, sad, and ready to get off the world at the next stop.

Now she was at this party smiling, joyful, and seemingly
reborn. She introduced Arnie and me to the source of her
delight, her second husband. She and Jessie had been married for three glorious months, and they felt the fates had
predestined this union. We, in our 44th year of connubial
bliss, could remember some three-month periods of such
euphoria, too.

This marriage sounded so good I feared my husband was
thinking the unspeakable thoughts I was thinking: This is
too good to be true. Does she protest too much? How long
can this living on cloud nine last?

The next day I ran the incident by a group of six women
friends to take a poll about second marriages.

Each of the six women knew six others who were involved

6

the second and third time around. Some had been divorced, some widowed. Some tied the knot firmly in the presence of clergy and family, others made promises in privacy to love, honor, and cherish.

Many of the women who were married more than once spoke of "The Real Husband," and that was not necessarily an endearing term. It connoted that man who made the real impact on the woman's life. It was the nomenclature given to the father of her children. One, in her fourth marriage, regretted she didn't work harder at the first.

Upon further study, revelations were exposed about the first mate being the romantic. He was handsome, suave and debonair.

"We were young, and though we didn't know just what love meant, we were 'In Love'," said Rita, twice widowed.

"It probably had more to do with biology, sociology, and geography than with any other factor," Ernestine said. She had been widowed once, divorced once, and is now single. "The maturity of our bodies and readiness for mating, the societal demand that we couple up, and where we were at the time, were responsible for whom we married."

The second time around, we're more sober, we hope.

"It's different, but it's the same," one 58-year-old bride fumbles for an explanation. "I thought I knew what to guard against. My first husband was laid back, kind of dull. So this time I chose the life of the party. He tells his jokes in public, but at home he's the same pouting little boy that my first husband was."

"When I married for the first time it was under the influence of blind passion," a 64-year-old woman confesses.

"Our mores of the times were such that we couldn't go to bed without the sanctity of wedlock. We felt committed to overlook the foreshadowing of problems that inevitably arose. It was our marriage, etched in stone, and it was the responsibility of both to hold it together.

Singles of mature years don't have as many choices. Physical lust, though present, is not the blinding drive it was in youth. "What is there to choose from?" asks an attractive recent widow, reciting an old wartime song, "They're either too young or too old; they're either too gray or too grassy green..."

Some say, "I have enough problems with my own children, why take on another family and its troubles?"

The woman looks for patience, not a patient. The man looks for a nurse, or someone willing to nurture him in his waning years. They've each had the good years—the virile, exciting, healthy, tolerant, accepting, strong, working years—with the first spouse. Now, the old song continues, "The pickings are poor, and the crop is lean..."

Yet, left widowed or divorced, many men and women in the Third Third would rather compromise and find a mate than remain single. "The worst husband is better than no husband," is the slogan of those who feel insecure being alone in a society of couples. The U.S. Census Bureau tells that the stigma of singlehood has been removed, and that remaining unattached is now acceptable to a growing number each year.

After the first mate is gone, lost to divorce, death, or desertion, that mate develops a halo in the mind's eye of the remaining spouse. Former problems evaporate into fond memories of the good times.

Only the current roommate's needs seem like inconsiderate demands that are beyond the call of marital duty. "Why can't he be more like my first husband?" is a frequent lament.

Marriage for the second time is a risky business, more so because we've tempered emotions and brought reason to decision making. It's more chancey, and more hazardous.

But, it's so nice to have a man around the house.

Hearts & Flowers
Don't Say It All

♦

Another Valentine's Day is being hyped, and I'm filtering my view of the occasion through my Third Third history. There's something artificial about the store displays that announce the "season of love." There's something saccharin and puerile about buying into that.

Years ago, when we first received our acculturation as Americans, we were taught as first graders that we sent a card to those children in the classroom whom we liked. Young as we were, I suspect we would have made the choice honestly. But, to not upset the teacher, our mothers made sure we brought to class an adequate number of cards for every child in the room.

Both of these women mentors were teaching us that in our society we are kind, concealing our true feelings, and outwardly generous. Even if Henry pulled my pigtails every chance he had; even if Sally danced so gracefully on her tippy toes; even if Ethel took the cookie from my lunch; even they must be rewarded with a "love" card.

The more mature we became, the more adjusted to living

9

in our society, the more we learned to not express our feelings. "Don't wear your heart on your sleeve," was the message of successful human interrelationships. We learned to smooth the edges of our attractions or repulsions toward others, to not rise so high with the peaks of emotion, nor fall to such depths.

Now, commercially, we're urged to "love, love, love" with the implicit promise that we will be "loved" in return. If I send you a red heart card, perhaps you will do the same for me, then I won't be lonely or feel like a reject. This attitude, my Third Third accumulation of experiences hints to me, is largely resposible for the difficulty young people have today in making lasting relationships.

Those who "fall in love" so superficially and tenuously, tend to "fall out of love" with as much ease.

Expecting hearts and flowers and feeling dejection if that symbolism is not forthcoming, is a frequent ailment of our times. It is exacerbated by such holidays as Valentine's Day and by the notion that romance comes packaged and is for sale. Along with that sales pitch is the one that everyone must be coupled. The messages don't say you can be a worthwhile human being even if you are not "in love" with someone and don't, perish the thought, receive a card or other stereotypical manufactured token.

Could it be that in our day, with all the sophisticated communications capabilities to choose from, we have trouble telling each other of our feelings and have to resort to a mass-printed card to convey our innermost tender expressions? Buying love by buying gifts is a flimsy coverup for someone who can't just come out and declare devotion. Lovers in days of old may have known something that has been lost in the fast lane, that sweet nothings can have as much impact whispered as sung; a scribbled note can be as endearing as a billboard sign declaring eternal fealty.

Over the years of being around to observe the "love"

affairs of the many, it seems the measurement of attentiveness does not necessarily reflect the inner feeling of one partner for another. Lil, who tends Ben in and out of his wheelchair, probably won't get or give a box of candy. Sam, who takes the baby's 3 a.m. feeding, may be a more caring lover than Tom, who skywrites a public declaration of his love for Terry.

I know a man who never remembers to prepare a card, or give flowers or perfume, or any of the other traditional signs that say, "I love you." He only took his wife out for an ice cream soda, and said he was happy to be married to her for 45 years.

And I liked it.

Partner For Life

◆

Age differences show up when we are the only people in the Third Third at a reception for Shawn and Mady who are about to be married.

The quips about "taking the plunge" are sent up like trial balloons, but fall away to empty grins among this gathering of young marrieds, who sense how precarious the situation is.

As if to bolster himself, the prospective groom says, "Not to worry. The Mitchels are role models." But, he looks scared, as rightfully he should be.

On the ride home, Arnie and I wonder if our 46 years of marriage do, indeed, qualify us as role models. We disagree and get into an argument, but we are old hands at differences of opinion.

OK, we'll consider endurance as a fair measurement of success. The first 40 years are the most difficult. It does get better as you go along, as you yield to the inevitable.

We do agree that couples about to march down the aisle are justified in being frightened by this dangerous venture.

The warning flag waves caution with statistics that tell of one out of two marriages ending in divorce. The ice is thin, but how shall they skate without falling in? Carefully.

Silent questions lurk in the subconscious.

Will he take care of the needed oil changes for her car as her father did? Will she prepare turkey dinner with nut stuffing like his mother does?

Will he turn out to be a couch potato as he slips into the comfort of home? Will she hang on the phone with girl friends when he wants her near?

Will he become less neat about his dressing? Will she spend less time on her makeup? Will he keep the cat off the table? Will she pull over to her side of the garage?

Will he allow her to develop as a person or will he expect her to confine herself to serving the family? Will she accept his career limitations even though he's not as ambitious as her sister's husband?

Will he want children enough to share in their care and development? Will she be patient with kids and raise them responsibly? Will they remain loyal partners over those bumps in the road which we of the Third Third know are out there? The answers to all of the above are yes and no. There are no assurances, no guarantees. The joy of living is in the living.

The current wisdom, in a time when there is a dearth of wisdom about marriage, is that those who are "successful" are those who remain themselves. Problems begin when each one expects the union to be perfect; perfection defined differently by each, according to background and expectations and beliefs in what's right and wrong.

For us it was tough when we saw each other at dinner time. I wanted him to understand that I was home with kids who were rambunctious after two weeks of confinement with the chicken pox. He needed me to sense his frustration that the snow impeded his business dealings.

Our malaise was not the marriage, but the tremendous trifles of life which we all face as long as there is life. All we needed of each other was understanding and caring.

It's like two people leaning against each other for support, when one moves, the other slips. If they aren't ready, the other falls unnecessarily. Prepared, with realistic expectations, they cope.

It's a big responsibility laid on us, that of being role models. The old goat says he holds my hand so he won't hit me; I accept that as the tender remark of a man preserving his macho image.

Even though I am so close to perfect, he's confessed he occasionally wanted to trade me in. Not me; I'm still hoping he will take my advice so he can become more perfect.

It must have been someone in the Third Third who coined the cliché about considering murder very often; divorce only 46 times.

Don't Buy
Green Bananas

◆

My trip to New York City last month was not so much for theater, museums, or sightseeing as it was to visit Uncle Jack. He had sounded so woebegone on the phone, and it worried me that he was living alone at 86. His wife, my aunt, died three years ago. My concern for him from afar did not take into account that we become more realistic with age.

I was pleasantly surprised to find him alert and perky. His apartment was neat and bright. He offered lunch from a well-stocked refrigerator. He seemed comfortable and content.

"You're doing so well," I said. "Next thing we know, you'll have a girl friend."

"Yes," he answered, blushing. "She'll be here to meet you in half an hour."

She arrived on schedule, a handsome, well-groomed, self-assured woman, also in her 80s. It was delightful to see how playful they were. Age didn't seem an obstacle to their forming a solid bond. Telling an inside joke, they giggled like any teenage couple alone together.

She introduced herself and told about her children, grandchildren, widowhood, career and other pertinent history. She concluded by saying, "Time is short, we were both lonely, and we need each other." I won't be surprised if I receive a marriage announcement in the near future.

Time is short. Seize the day. Long-range planning in the late part of the Third Third is inappropriate. Older people better understand the fullness of living with death close at hand.

At that age, they don't buy green bananas.

Once, when my mother was in her late 70s, we talked about her schedule for the next day. She was planning to attend the funeral of a friend in the morning and to play bridge in the afternoon.

"How can you be so insensitive?" I asked.

She explained, without apology, that death is so common an occurrence in her peer group that if they called off their card game each time someone died, they would be perpetually mourning.

"Besides," she added, "the older we get, the more we accept death as a reality of living. We're happy for the day we're alive, not bed-bound, not having to 'doctor'."

If they can make it to whatever is fun, to be with friends, to form relationships, to enjoy each day, that's living. Every morning is serendipitous.

It was a lesson for me about the facts of life.

I recall a flippant condo joke about the widows preparing a roast-chicken dinner to keep in the freezer when one of the women in their building was taken to the hospital.

"She's on her last legs," the story went. "He'll miss his wife of 53 years. But he'll need to have dinner the night that she dies."

Last week I attended the funeral of an 85-year-old woman who had been married for 61 years. It was touching, even to those of us who were not close to the family, when her

90-year-old husband bent over the open bier to kiss her goodbye.

Later that week, when he was asked whether he would remain in the apartment alone or live with his children, he was quick to respond. He seemed to have thought about it.

"I'll investigate the singles scene," he answered.

I suspect he won't have a long research project. The frozen roasted chicken dinners are waiting.

To Get Closer,
You Get Away

♦

I f we make it to our 46th wedding anniversary, it will be thanks to my recent trip—three weeks away from husband and home. Our marriage survives better with occasional spaces in our relationship.

Each year we have a dialogue that goes like this:

I (around March 15): "This year let's plan our vacation early."

He (deeply engrossed in opening game of the baseball season or a golf tournament or a tennis match): "Sure."

I (after reading an enticing story in the travel section, or when the first brochure arrives): "Look at the wonderful bargain to. . ."

He (genuinely puzzled): "Why? We have such a nice home, good food, new mattress. Why do you want to leave all the goodies that everyone struggles a lifetime to achieve?"

I (batting my eyelashes): "I want to be cooked for, served. I want to have my bed made, to see new places."

He (using that old lure that I used to bite but now, with the experience of age, don't even nibble at): "You know you're the best cook in the world. Neither of us really likes a three-week diet of restaurant food. Besides, at our age we can't digest all the junk they serve."

I (firmly): "All my life I've worked to achieve three weeks out of the kitchen. I can't stand the heat."

He (with great sincerity): "OK, I'll cook."

After the third TV dinner, second meal of hot dogs and beans, and second pizza in one week, we simultaneously come to the agreement that in the fall I'll go off to see the world while he enjoys the comforts of home.

My big concession is to stock the freezer with interesting food, easily microwaved. After all, I do want him to survive.

Finding a friend with the same set of circumstances who wants to see the same part of the world is not too difficult.

Returning from this year's trip to Russia, I had a twinge of remorse even though I had enjoyed the experience. I had missed him. I also felt uncomfortable traveling without a man to get me to rest when there was more to see, to argue with authority about an overcharge and to help carry the luggage.

Generally, I longed for my comfortable home, my kitchen, my territory and my husband.

From the moment he picked me up at the airport, he was attentive and adoring.

He: "I was lonely. Next year I'll come with you."

I: "No. Next year I won't go."

We lovingly promise that next year will be different. We smooch and behave like young lovers for at least a week. Until the fall football lineup.

This year, hearing rumblings of a football strike on my return, I had hopes that fate would weigh the scales in my favor. How had the women of America accomplished that in my absence?

But it was a short-lived fantasy. Radical change does not come that easily. The baseball season continues, and there are re-runs of past years' football victories to relive and war movies to revisit.

My husband is again planted in his favorite position, zapping the TV channels, eating "the best food in the world" and sleeping on the most comfortable mattress.

And I don't mind. There's much I want to catch up with since my vacation. And I'm sure, from past experience, that he will take time away from the TV, no matter what is happening there, to celebrate our anniversary on October 13th.

Left Behind Is Lonely

♦

Shirley and Sidney; Sidney and Shirley. That's the way they were. Two halves of a whole. Interdependent. Married for more than 50 years, their lives were a "we." In the 15 years I knew them, they were a pair. Until last week.

Sidney died at 71.

In the Third Third, we are acutely aware that everyone goes. We understand that death is part of life. We surely know no one is immortal.

Sidney was a mortal man. That was his charm. He was Mr. Average American Joe.

He was a nice guy, a *jai alai aficionado*.

He was involved with cars: fixing them, selling them. He was humble. He was a doting grandfather. He was the best darned Lindy-hopper I've ever seen.

He fulfilled life's cycle. Born to a poor family, he worked hard and brought his own family up to a middle-class standard. He had a *joie de vivre* and smiled a lot. He was stricken with cancer and fought courageously, and uncomplainingly, until the dying of the light. What more can a person ask?

He lived, he loved, he died. It's not unusual. It's not tragic. It's not dramatic. It happens to all of us. And that's what, in the Third Third, is hovering over us, threatening us.

We hear the bell tolling, and pause to wonder for whom. We hear the distant ring as a knelling reminder that it is coming closer. We know that nobody knows when.

Knowing that if it happened to Shirley, it could happen to us, we accelerate our pace and go on to enjoy what time we have left. It will happen to us. It brings couples closer than ever before.

What will happen to the one left behind? After so many years, a marriage becomes, for better or for worse, an entity. The many elements that have been cemented into the marriage shape a structure, like a house, that settles into its own form. When one leaves, taking along parts of that structure, the entire thing crumbles.

Shirley will make it. She is a strong lady. She told us not to cry. She was rational and understood that it was inevitable.

She has her loving memories of their years together. He was her first teenage love; he was her lover.

She has children and grandchildren nearby and a circle of friends built up from living in the same community for so long. She has her golf and her home and her bowling and her needlepoint.

No, she didn't cry. But it broke my heart to see her so alone.

It must be awful to have to start an entirely new life at this advanced age. It must be devastating to begin to find a way to fill the space and the time that Sid occupied every day. It must be bewildering to turn around to say something to him and suddenly remember that he isn't there anymore, and never will be.

That's reality. It happens to every relationship, sooner or later, and never at the right time.

We bury the dead and after a while, a short while if we're lucky, we turn to living. And life goes on.

Easy for me to say.

The Long, Wonderful
Road To 50 Years

♦

The song, *I'm In The Mood For Love,* drew us, in our Third Third, onto the dance floor, comfortable with "our music."

We had gathered to celebrate the 50th wedding anniversary of longtime friends. They looked so right fox-trotting, Ruth and Jack, that I had to shake myself into reality, brought only into the here and now by their gray hair. The years melted away; they don't show the effects. Theirs are smiles of contentment. Out of earshot of the other, they each said, "It's been great."

What motivated all these people to come together for this occasion, traveling an aggregate of over 100,000 miles? One daughter came from Germany, another from Colorado, a granddaughter from Texas, relatives and friends from Arizona, California, and many from the northeast. Is it just that this couple has endured for 50 years in these times when relationships are so fragile and short lived? Partly.

When I first met Ruth, she and I maneuvered baby carriages on upper Broadway in New York City, the unlikely and uncomfortable temporary location for us during World War II. We waited, daily, for word that our husbands were safe. Each man, unknown to the other, was in the heat of battle in Europe. Her carriage was a perambulator built for lovely, identical twin daughters.

"Where did the years go?" is the eternal question of those in the Third Third. Where, indeed? My husband and I had kept our eye on them constantly. "I can't remember getting older, when did they?"

Our paths, over the years, often paralleled, sometimes crossed. When they were on Long Island, we were in New Jersey. They moved to Kentucky. We moved to Ohio. We kept in touch. Now we are, in the later years, here together.

He started his career stuffing cigarette machines and gradually, one pack at a time, moved forward into the vending machine industry, ending his career as president of a TWA subsidiary.

"I could rely on him to take good care of us." smiles Ruth, proudly today, in retrospect, with the same cheerful attitude about the future she had even during the war.

"She fit me like a glove," he glows. "I thought we would be a good pair in 1938, and I was right. It's been more than we could have expected."

Although we never heard of any deep disagreements they had, surely their road together had bumps like the rest of ours. Long marriages are like a multifaceted diamond. Each year, each shared experience, for better or for worse, cuts across the stone at another angle, rendering the ultimate product brilliant, glowing, sparkling in the light of examination. A jewel.

To look back is to come across the joys of building together, of raising a family that in turn went out to make a place in the world.

Fifty years of living with anyone, especially a beloved one, creates a unique relationship that supercedes the rest of the world. There are friends in common, ambitions failed or achieved, compromises that allow each to feel like a winner, knowledge of each others habits and vulnerabilities, joys and sorrows. Five decades of togetherness become two individuals living one life. "But," says Ruth, the patient, the supportive, the solid both-feet-on-the-ground, "we began and developed lots of interests in common, but allowed for separate interests."

That's a big statement about a couple who played in bridge tournaments together, an arena of conflict for many couples. They each play with a different partner.

Toasts to the best parents in the world, the best brother in the world, the best business partner and the best friends are offered by people who followed the marriage year by year and came together for the party to congratulate Ruth and Jack for setting an example.

The young people don't dance; they seem to not relate to our music. The young people seem to be awed by the magnitude of a half century of marriage to the same person. But Ruth and Jack say, "It's wonderful."

As we hear the strains of the *Anniversary Waltz* and see the gray-haired dancers in each other's arms, we understand the reason for the celebration.

A Time To Mourn–
A Time To Live

♦

We buried Fran seven months ago and it was sad.
There were many people whose lives were
lessened by her death.

Mostly Stan, her husband of 41 years. Stan clung to us
after the funeral, knowing that we too felt her loss, albeit
not as deeply as he did.

At first he was preoccupied with the day-by-day task of
closing up her life. The painful process of sorting the
plethora of personal things that are now memories is an
inevitable, distressful task we in the Third Third leave for
each other.

Then Stan spoke about the haunting feeling of walking
through their home, wanting to share something, turning
to look for her, and the thundering awareness that she
would not answer, then or ever.

He enrolled in a "grief group" where, together with others
going through the early stages of loss, he shared feelings and
means of coping, taking each day in its course. We encouraged him, knowing, generally, that eventually time heals.

Soon he would joke about learning the art of being single. He told us about his failed and successful attempts at cooking. He called once to ask how often he should clean the inside of the refrigerator and couldn't believe my answer: "When it doesn't pass the nose test."

He was making a good adjustment despite his continuous tearful tales about his loneliness.

We recalled my father, sorrowful and mournful, when my mother died after 60 years of marriage. Arnie, my husband, would tease him: "You have no one to quarrel with."

"Don't kid yourself, my boy," Papa would respond. "That's an important part of marriage, and I miss it."

In our wisdom gleaned from other widowers, we felt Stan would make the transition and eventually meet another woman with whom he could share life.

He is healthy, handsome, well-to-do and charming. Three months after being widowed, he was invited to dinner by married friends with lone women acquaintances to even out the seating. Women, widowed and divorced, invited him to their homes. "Come for dinner and stay for breakfast," some boldly put it.

He dated. He didn't kiss and tell, but he reported the awkwardness of being a man older than 60 who is unfamiliar with the dating scene of today.

"Should I bring candy or a bottle of wine when she invites me to dinner?" "What kind of corsage is appropriate to bring to my date for her class reunion?"

We noted a tinge of boyish excitement coupled with the older man's bewilderment about these social occasions.

My husband's interest was inordinately piqued. He shared the concerns with Stan and his pleasure when, after a date, he told of being nervous about where to go, what to say, whether to ask that woman out for a third time lest it would seem too rushed.

Last week Stan called his four married children and then

us to announce he had found his new mate, and that they would be getting married within a few weeks. He had mourned hard if not long.

The bride is very beautiful and about 20 years Stan's junior. She has three teenage kids. And he's as happy as a bridegroom is supposed to be.

"Cluck, cluck, cluck," went the tongues of all our peers who know Stan. "Ain't it awful. . ." It's too soon. He will act in haste, repent at leisure. He is taking on a chore of raising young children. He would be better off to marry a more mature woman, one closer to the age of his former wife, not just five years older than his daughter.

Arnie can't get enough of the talk. He rallies to the discussion of the November-May relationship. With a lascivious grin he tells the tired joke about the older man who wears out the younger woman. "If she can't keep up with him, that's her problem," he chortles.

I'm feeling strangely uncomfortable, and I don't know why.

New Morality
In The Third Third

♦

It's a new day a-dawning.

It's a new day when Merle is brazenly living with a man without benefit of clergy, for all the world to know. Merle and her lover are in their Third Third.

Oh dear, and perish to Betsy! You mean they're having an affair?

For two years, Merle and Ed kept it secret so no one would know, especially her children, who were sure to disapprove. The concept of their mother in such a casual living arrangement is shocking to people in the younger generation who view their parents as having high moral standards that preclude extramarital affairs. It's also shocking to many of the couple's contemporaries.

Now that they appear at social and family gatherings as a couple, Merle defends her position to her friends. She met Ed shortly after her husband died following a three-year illness.

She had been emotionally depressed after seeing her first love, the father of her children, fade before her eyes. She was physically exhausted from caring for him. She was mentally drained from being out of touch with society and the futility of it all.

Ed was a breath of fresh air. He took her out of her home and her doldrums. He hadn't known her past life, nor she his, which put them into a new forward focus. She didn't wish her husband to die, but she must go on.

"My kids wouldn't have been any more pleased if I had gone into heavy mourning and became a widow in black. I might have been a burden to them," Merle says. "I have a chance at 62 for many years ahead. Why wait?"

OK, then get married. But Merle and Ed see no advantage.

Some people decide to marry for the purpose of having children.

"As soon as I suspect I'm pregnant," Merle chuckles, "I'll agree to marry him."

Disagreements among second-time-around couples come to the fore when one feels too much attention and money is given to the other's children, especially when their funds are combined. As singles, when their monies are held separately, the problem is avoided.

The federal government precipitated the phenomenon of older people losing their inhibitions and living together. A woman who has not worked steadily enough to have accumulated Social Security on her own is eligible for her husband's share when she is widowed.

Until recently, if she married, she would have had to relinquish that source of independent income. To many couples, that didn't make sense.

Now the law has changed and, under most conditions, if she's older than 60, she's able to receive her husband's Social Security benefits without penalty for her lifetime, whether or not she remarries.

What about declaring a commitment to each other? Today

they share the living responsibilities; he picks up his clothes, helps with the shopping, does the dishes.

She does the cooking and other household chores. Merle observes other second marriages where, once the honeymoon is over, all of their comforts and needs become hers to implement. Men of this age prefer the security of a caretaker.

"Besides, we're older now," Merle says. "We've become more practical. Like the last sweet strawberry of the season, we want to squeeze the juice, the joy of life, as much as we can."

Then, thoughtfully, she says, "I don't want to become a nurse to another man, and at our age, that's a possibility."

Isn't the commitment to care for him the same, married or not? She doesn't know now. "We'll see."

"Meantime, I like this permanent courting arrangement. He still brings me flowers, and I'd like to keep it that way as long as I can."

This is a sign of our times as we cut new paths in the Third Third.

Tender Tangled Vines

◆

A Vacation Is A Real
Test Of Family Ties

◆

The children are coming. The children are coming. What transplanted parent of adult children has not felt a quickened pulse at the sound of that cry?

I have been subjected to endless hours of friends' detailed accounts of exaggerated achievements of their progeny, seen through rose-tinted bifocals. At long last, it's my turn. Our son and daughter and their respective spouses are coming with our four grandchildren.

My husband and I have consciously and conscientiously chosen not to pace our existence to the rhythm of our offspring. We gave them life and it's theirs to live. We birthed them, nourished them, educated them, and with the toughest act of love, separated from them.

We migrated to Florida with the satisfaction of having accomplished our role as parents. We launched them on their respective ways with our blessings. We have fulfilling lives here that welcome their presence, but we do not need them.

We know the joy of paper families, seeing through letters and pictures the next generation of four beautiful buds

35

opening to the sunshine, each with colorful personality and individual pursuit.

But we paid a price as they reached each stage of growth.

We were not with them when our son decided to change careers, or when our daughter's family chose their home.

We missed the sweet-16 party, cheering at the Little League games and the recital of the Suzuki-taught violinist, the packing for the first scouting overnight.

But now I stand in the grocery line with an overflowing cart because tomorrow the children are coming.

Can we spend the three weeks together aware of the hierarchy of generations without invoking parental power? Will they slip easily into the comfort of our home, although Florida has never been their home? Is our used-to-be family foursome of love elastic enough to stretch for inclusion of 10?

I wonder if they'll open up in this brief visit to share their concerns and be interested in ours? I wonder if we have overexpectations of each other? I wonder if they harbor resentments for real or imagined inequities in their up-bringing, or if they'll hug us for their roots in warm soil that nourished their growth to the fine adults they are.

Can we be kind and gentle to each other? Can we be helpful, but not interfering? Can we not take each other for granted? Can we refrain from offering an opinion on every subject? Can we seal our lips on aches and problems they cannot relieve?

Will they sense that although we are active, age has insidiously crept upon us and we justifiably fear incapacitation? Will we be demanding of their youth and vitality? Will we show signs of the real disease of aging, self-centeredness.

While they're here, we'll enjoy Epcot Center and the Discovery Center and favorite dishes from Mom's kitchen. We'll visit Lockhart Stadium, the Davie horse farms and the skating rink in Sunrise, maybe go water skiing in

Quiet Waters park. And all along the way, we'll share laughter.

My mother, insistent that her grown children travel to South Florida annually from Ohio, used to say, "I'm happy to see your faces, and then happy to see your backs." And that's OK. I understand. But right now I'm putting my life here on hold, and tonight I won't sleep—the children are coming, the children are coming.

Searching Mall And
Soul For Perfect Gifts

♦

The hot Florida sun argues with the calendar that says it's December and time to shop. My mother's saying, "There's many a mile from a grandmother's heart to a granddaughter's smile," comes back to me in my dilemma about what appropriate token to buy, especially for my three granddaughters. I don't really know you.

There's a special place that each child holds in the un-questioning, accepting love of the grandparent for the many reasons we understand, not the least of which is the prom-ise of a continuation of one's self: life beyond life.

The miles between us have condemned me to missing the pleasure of watching and participating in the day-to-day development and flowering of the unique you. Would we have a closer rapport if we were physically closer? Despite the phone company ads, that would have us believe one can reach and touch someone, for me the reach is a strain.

All three of you granddaughters are teenagers now. I vow to you, I try to raise my consciousness to you in the here and now, and not as I fondly remember you—soft, gurgling, cuddly babies, or until age 10, responsive to attention and yielding to my need for touching. Reflections of too few times spent with you deepens those events into meaningful experiences for me to cling to.

Between our meetings, you the outgoing one, are fixed in my inner vision as a humanist who helps because she cares about her mother being tired from a day's work. The sounds of you I remember are a giggle in your serious attempts at violin virtuosity. You knocked my socks off when you were named most valuable player by your softball team.

You, the sensitive beauty of the family. Where did you get your looks, kid? I can't claim a link in that genetic chain, but I'm delighted you found those profound eyes. I know that outer beauty you present to the world has the depth it suggests.

And you, Alice in Wonderland, move about in the same wondering, wandering way. Unspoiled. I hope the jolt of losing your innocence is not too painful. You read sophisticated books so avidly that it surprised me when you slipped through the crowd to privately kiss Mickey Mouse.

My three great hopes for tomorrow, I'm doomed to sublimation of my desire to know you and be part of your metamorphosis from cocoon to butterfly.

Reflecting on mother's myths, I recall bubbling into my grandmother's waiting arms and surrendering myself to her lengthy bear hug. "Oh, Gramma," I exploded. "Henry asked me to the prom!" "What's a prom?" asked the old woman whose lifestyle had not encountered that term. I tried to explain, to no avail. She patted my cheek and responded, "If it's good for you, it's good for me."

Still I agonize about what will have meaning to you as a gift of love. I offer you passion for life; excitement in each day. I transmit to you a sense of your opportunities for fulfillment as a person based on the good standards you already have, not on what you think the world demands of you. I wish you self-confidence to welcome challenges and solve them creatively. I dispatch to you the courage to trade negative emotions for new ideas which you will evaluate and use to advantage. I impart to you the pursuit to become a woman of substance behind the pretty face. Mostly, I give to you the awareness that you have before you a vast lifetime of choices and, though freedom is the most difficult of human concepts to deal with, I wish that for each of you.

Probably, at the end of this mall-searching and soul-searching for the appropriate present for you, I'll forward something as mundane as a sweater, or a greenback, which is always the right size and color. You'll have to take the will for the deed.

And, like my grandmother, I too will have to settle for a brief peripheral touch with your life, and carry with me the unknowing, but joyful feeling of your joys.

The Passing of Saul

◆

Pop is 95 and Mom is 92. He puts her shoes on for her because she gets dizzy when she bends over. She holds him up when he shakes from a neurological problem. She sees fine; he hears well. Together my in-laws make a whole person.

Arnie, their older child, my husband, is 66. They have been married a year more than that. Pop tells us that he is fading, and that the doctors are out to take his resources away. When we try to quiet him, he will say, "Oh, what do you kids know?" We react by feeling young, but angry.

They have their own apartment in an adult congregate living facility where meals are prepared and a person bathes them and gives the personal care they need. One or both of us visits them twice a week, and speaks to them more often. "Why can't you spend more time with us?" Pop asks. "You kids don't know how lonely it is to be old."

As we enter their apartment we hear the flutter of the wings of the dark angel. But when I'm feeling my age, I'm convinced Pop will be limping at my funeral.

Pop can't see, but he picked up the nickel he spotted on the floor. Mom is senile, but still enjoys having a manicure.

He watches soap operas, but complains that she no longer understands the stories, or anything. And it's true. She doesn't recognize her grandchildren, but tells in detail about her Bolivian boyfriend from before she was married.

Pop is demanding of everyone around him but equally of himself. There is no pleasing him or satisfying his demands. He's tough because life is tough.

I met him 45 years ago, this man with whom my life has been inextricably intertwined. We've quarreled frequently, perplexing those who witness our butting wills. We challenged each other for my husband, the man we both love, whom he never relinquished. Only he and I know the love and mutual respect we had, notwithstanding.

He takes a cab to the hospital and has himself admitted. He leaves just as impetuously explaining, "Mom needs me."

He with unsmiling high resolve, would say, "Girls are much more difficult to raise. That's why we had two boys."

By sheer force of will, without skills, he made a living for his family and put away for his old age. When business was slow in his retail store, that rough, tough cream puff would escape to play in his rose garden.

Dissatisfied with our lack of cooperation in transporting him, he learned to drive at age 53. People in Dover, N.J. still remember clearing the road for him.

His mind is as keen as when I first met him, but it hasn't found him many ways to pleasure. "What do you youngsters know of what I've been through?" he starts to tell of growing up in a village in Poland. "Hard. Hard."

One of eight children, he knew what hunger was. "My father liked me best," he told. "I was the hardest worker. But when he caught me ice skating in a pond behind the mill, he beat me to a pulp. That was when I vowed to run away to America." He was 14 and never saw his father again. "I never really laughed much after that," he said.

But I caught him once. During World War II, as my husband was trapped at the Battle of the Bulge, I spotted Pop with his first grandchild rolling on the floor gleefully playing with a jumping frog toy. The joy of that scene remains etched in my memory, and probably in both of theirs. He laughed several more times with the oncoming grandchildren, but was quick to cover up with a show of stoicism.

He is tenacious. Like so many frail elderly, just waking up in the morning is a chore. The bodily functions become exhausting. And he hasn't yet told any of us that he loves us, but we all know it.

Years ago, when I took Mom to the beauty parlor he would call it frivolous, and she would timidly agree that his haircutting was just as good. Last week he asked to have her taken to a salon. It's as if he hears the grim reaper knocking at his door. In his usual commanding way, he wants to be in charge and make all the arrangements.

How can he put down his joust when Mom needs him? How can he trust the future to us kids who just don't know?

But yesterday, even Saul Mitchel did.

Miles-Away-Mothers

◆

Usually an "up" person, Milly returned from her trip "down." At first she didn't identify the problem, and I let it go, thinking it was only my imagination that the week-long visit with her children had been less gratifying than anticipated.

Over lunch, I brought up the subject again. She had found her children and grandchildren cordial, kind, courteous.

"I suppose, all that I could ask for," she reported. "Then why did I feel so cold?"

All of us mothers in this mobile society, who live far-flung from our children, place great stock in such visits; one week to last a year. We feel we must cram all the love and all the intergenerational connection into a small space of time.

In one week, we do not get below the surface conversation with our own children, especially if they are married. Our fear of interfering in their lives keeps us from talking about anything deeper than the most superficial subjects.

"They care," Milly said, searching for her inner feelings, "but from a distance."

We acknowledge that out-of-sight is out-of-mind. But we are seeking from them a caring similar to that which we have for them. We agree that as miles-away-mothers we want to live our independent lives, and are pleased that our offspring have found a place for themselves.

But we'd like the tie to be a little more short and taut, rather than so loose and languid.

Milly, 15 years a widow, has adapted well because she saw no alternatives. She is a self-sufficient woman, as are so many of us in the Third Third.

We don't cling to our children. We don't depend on them for our everyday welfare. They are free to laugh and cry as adults, living in their beds as they make them. But, she wants her grown-up and grown-away child to ask, "How ya' doin', Mom?" and be ready for the answer, pleasing or problematic.

I recall several years ago when I broke my shoulder. My daughter's reaction, when she first heard about it was, "I know my mom, she'll be back on the tennis court in a week."

True, she displayed confidence in my recuperative powers and she felt I was strong enough to not need her. But who doesn't need a little extra loving in times of hurt? Was she, rather, saying that she didn't want to be needed?

We speculate and wonder if we are remiss in not leaning on our children more. Why be so protective of their leisure and be so undemanding of their responsibility to us?

"Should it have been my concern if my daughter-in-law didn't want to come for family dinner with regularity when we lived nearby?" Milly asked. "Instead of withdrawing the request, I could have made my wishes known and left it to my son to deal with."

The permissiveness with which we raised our children, today's baby boomers, is boomeranging on us. We were casual in our teachings about filial bonds, and they are casual in response.

Gone are the days when family ties were immutable, solid, unquestionable. Now elders must "earn" and "deserve" their kids' love, as if the kids were always lovable, earning and deserving of their parents' unqualified acceptance.

Gone are the days for us stiff-necked parents who don't want to admit to needing a small return of tender loving care, to expect voluntary attention. It's too late, at this stage to change the pattern of interrelationships, to create a mandatory, obligatory show of affection.

Parents are the strong ones. They are always there to heal the hurts: invincible, invulnerable. Forever there.

We wonder if it works. Does the mother who brings over a prepared chicken so the daughter won't have to cook get a more heartfelt invitation to dinner? Does the father who helps with the mortgage payments on the house get a bigger smile? Is buying indeed tying?

Or are the relationships in families where the offspring were given love, food, clothing, shelter and an education while they were at home, then turned loose to live life on their own, basically just as solid?

Do the miles-away-mothers have to settle for modified affection from distant children with whose lives they are not intricately intertwined? Have the independent parents released the next generation from a soft, gentle tie, if not a strong, binding cable by not requiring attention?

There's got to be a half-way, moderate level of family relationships.

Milly had a good time with her family. She came back to where she works, plays and lives out the rest of her life alone. But she's putting a note in her vault so they'll find it with the inheritance her children may look for when she's gone.

The note will say, "I survived. But I was lonely for you."

Memories Of Father Make
Father's Day Memorable

◆

This is the first Father's Day of my 64-year life in which I'm without a father, and it evokes a lifetime of memories and emotions. I'll try not to be sad, for Papa always told me to look forward.

Sorting through my memorabilia, I find many father's fables and foibles.

He was a dignified man, and vain. I see him always in my store of images in white shirt, tie, fedora, and with his clipped moustache. He was the quintessential gentleman; tipping his hat and offering a gallant phrase, even at 98, when he remembered very few people he met.

He was respected by all who knew him and sensed his self respect. He was known as Mr. Furman even, oddly enough, by my mother.

He was a well-liked and admired man. Once, when he was in the hospital, being treated for malnutrition as a result of his belief that people eat too much, it seemed that every one of the 400 workers of the factory he managed brought him homemade muffins or jam. I grew up in the reflected glory of being Mr. Furman's daughter.

He was deeply religious, although he didn't subscribe to much of the ritual. He based his life on the principle that the highest goal is the morality of everyday human-to-human relationships. "Who can know what's right or wrong?" he would answer a dilemma my brother or I was facing. "You start with the golden rule and temper it to real life. People are but a little lower than the angels. We are here to do God's work. Although no person can expect to complete it, no one is free to desist from starting." He spurred us to look forward.

He was a learned man. He believed his body was here only as support for his head, which he valued dearly. He was a pleasant person to be with, always ready with a philosophic message in a story, a joke, a song. "Life is to live," and he lived each day.

He was a self-made man, but was never a good earner. He shunned money and we got along. Orphaned at 5, he had to find the world for himself. He was always searching and pleased with his discoveries, sharing them enthusiastically: "Emerson said this; Tolstoy that." For fun he read Jack London and the comics.

He left no material estate except the books that he read avidly, especially the last 30 years of his life, hoping to catch up with the time spent working to support the family.

I remember the excitement of almost every evening's family dinner, when he would raise an issue that was on the front page of the paper and provoke a discussion. Often, he defended the least popular position for the sake of stimulating argument. Mama would plead for "one quiet meal" while we became embroiled in the pros and cons of the Works Progress Administration or the revolution in China.

Very angry with Papa, when I was 12, I greeted him at

Mom Is
Outside Looking In

♦

I t was not a matter of eavesdropping. The two women seated to the left of me were discussing their summer plans and their voices boomed through the small coffee shop.

The two were well-dressed, obviously in their Third Third. I gleaned from their talk that they were widows.

"A week is all I can stay at my son's," said the one in the pink blouse.

She began the oft-told tale of mothers who raise their children to maturity in their homes. Today, they don't feel comfortable in their adult child's home — not even for a short visit.

Both her son and daughter-in-law work intensively during the week. When Mama is there they try to limit their working hours and outside social involvement. But they come home tired and spent.

Her granddaughter is in high school. When she gets home she has to hit her books. There always seems to be an exam tomorrow.

"What should I do during the day when nobody's home?" Mama's voice has a tinge of the martyr.

"I try to help by offering to do some chores. I would shop or cook the meals for them. But they say, 'Mother, you're on vacation. You take it easy.'

"I don't want them to feel a burden, so I don't insist. Anyways, I would hesitate to mix into my daughter-in-law's household. You know the old saying. There's never a kitchen big enough for two women.

"So I sit around watching *As the World Turns* and *General Hospital* which I don't even do at home. I can't follow the stories. It's boring.

"When they finally get home I don't want to pounce on them, but I would like to chat with them. I can see they would like some privacy, but by then I can't wait to be with them, so, as much as I try not to show it, I'm impatient. After all, I'm only there one week out of 52.

"The sleeping arrangements are a problem. My granddaughter sleeps on the living room sofa when I'm there. She gives up her bed and room saying, 'Gramma, it's my pleasure.'

"I don't like to displace her. I hear her speaking to friends on the phone, and she tries to be cheerful when she tells them her grandmother is visiting and she can't join them. But I'm not so old fashioned that I don't understand that she would rather be with her peers.

"My daughter-in-law plans a barbecue in my honor and invites her parents over to join us. They talk about what happened the week before and about plans for two months away. I'm not around and can't participate. I feel like an outsider.

"I'm pleased that my son has a family arrangement in which he feels comfortable. They are all nice people. But I'm not one of that family. We live in two separate worlds.

"We're related, but we can't relate."

Her companion protests that, after all, mother is still the one who birthed and raised her son, and apparently he loves her or he wouldn't invite her to visit.

"I'm gratified that my son has such an apparently good marriage. In these days, when you hear of so many marital problems, I'm glad they get along."

Her friend, busily eating her lunch, nods in agreement.

"I'll come home after a week to where I belong," she says.

A Daughter Grown

♦

We've just returned from taking our daughter and her husband to the airport. They visited us for the weekend. It's startling to be reminded that the apple doesn't fall far from the family tree.

Madelaine has now, in maturity, at almost 45, just about reached perfection. She is a handsome woman, charming, polite and well mannered. Her values are good values. They are the values I value. She's great.

Now that I'm in the Third Third, I examine life, wondering who she and I are, what is our relationship, when did we become separated as mother and child, why do we see things eye to eye yet completely differently, and where did those odd genes come from?

Anything that I don't take credit for, I'll attribute to her father's heritage or environmental influence.

She is a late sleeper and feigns to be a lazy housekeeper. Where did she get those traits? Surely not from me.

She is more liberal with her children than I would be and I worry that they will be lacking in moral structure. The new mores are not mine, but time marches on, and I must accept the manners of today.

My daughter is intelligent, gregarious, an upstanding citizen. She, too, worries about what the world would be like if chocolate had not been invented. She's a chip off the old block.

But Madelaine is also a smoker and I'm concerned about her health. Although she grew up in a smoking home when we thought the weed was only harmless fun, I want to rescind that teaching. If I kicked the habit, why can't she?

She is a concerned mother and a supportive wife. I'm proud of the way she conducts her family life. There is little that supercedes her loyalty to the unit she has created. I applaud that.

She is an inattentive daughter. That must be because of our mobility, the way of today, a la Yuppie mode. Surely not anything I've done.

She is much more accepting of the world as she finds it than I am. She likes Michael Feinstein singing Irving Berlin music. Where did I go wrong?

She's concerned with growing old. I'm finding this time of my life so rewarding and want to celebrate the newfound years that I didn't expect would be here. She doesn't see us growing older or acknowledge our aging into antiquity. But she worries about her gray hairs. Did we find the road into middle age so full of hurdles?

She is non-competitive and non-conservative about money. How unlike me, the child of the Depression who grew up in the northeast, is she, the Baby Boomer from Ohio.

We share a taste in clothes, food, home decor, and humor. That's about all. But it's good to have a daughter to share even that with.

She is bubbly, effervescent like fresh champagne, and to be with her is heady and enjoyable. She is delightful and a constant source of pride and wonder for me. Her father just says about her plusses, "Of course."

I have wanderlust while she is afraid to fly. But as we kiss goodbye when she boards the plane for home and wonder when we will see each other again, I am filled with pride that I had a part in producing this woman, my daughter. Why not?

The apple doesn't fall far from the apple tree.

But I sometimes wonder what that orange is doing there?

Children Near and Far

♦

I t was the day after Mother's Day when I reported to my friend that Arnie and I had gone on our once-a-year fishing trip.

It was a nice day together, out on the water, away from it all, trying to determine whether the little pull at the line was a weed or a fish. I'd rather do that than hang out near the phone hoping to get a call from my children.

In my Third Third, I've learned to accept what I get. It takes the expectation out of my relationship with them.

My good friend is fortunate enough to have her children living nearby.

She did not want her name used because she shared with me some drawbacks in too much closeness.

There is an imposing awareness that my children are far and hers are near. It is the sort of unmentionable consciousness that would exist between us if she were wealthy and I were poor. We could be friends, but that delicate subject would be an acknowledged, yet unspoken fact of life, one we'd learn to live with and set aside.

"This way they don't feel guilty if they didn't call, nor am I angry because I don't know if they called," I explained. How thoroughly a modern mother can one be?

"It's not as great as it would seem on the surface," said my friend, almost defensively. Proximity brings problems, she explained.

Sure, it's warm and snug to be in the same community. Sure, it's comfortable to be with people you love and who love you. Sure, it rounds out the cutting edges of the world out there. They are together frequently.

But. . . she said she sees too much.

Her son-in-law, a physician, spends little time with his family. On Mother's Day, he picked away at his children's behavior. They could do nothing right, and father and family were constantly quarreling.

"A mother doesn't like to see that," she said. "Even though you know it may go on in everyone's home, still you don't like to be witness."

They don't really talk about things that matter. If anything they avoid sensitive topics. The family knows too much about you.

Her son is an acknowledged, incorrigible spendthrift. He never learned the value of a dollar, although his mother did not neglect the subject. He wanted everything in sight as he was growing up and now that he's out of the home and married, he hasn't changed. Everyone knows he's deep in debt, and there's nothing much left to say on the subject at a family gathering.

"But when he invites us to shop with him for a boat, it's aggravating," she said. "If you get together with family less frequently you don't see the warts as clearly."

There are expectations of each other. Everyone recalls negatives. One person starts a thought and the other knows what you're thinking and finishes the sentence. The younger kids play off one parent against the other. Members of the family speak with a lack of respect for each other. Parents hearing these quarrels are, in these days, worried about imminent divorce and are tempted to interfere and advise, further exacerbating the problem. Does familiarity breed contentment or contempt?

I think these negatives are far outweighed by the great joy of watching the grandchildren develop, having someone a local phone-call away on those days when you have a need to reach out, and the general togetherness that humans want.

In this mobile society, we're finding much freedom from the obligations of family life. Nor, as our kids grow up, do we want to stifle them with too much mothering. We want the world to be their oyster and tell them there is no limit to how high they can rise and where they can achieve their individual dreams. It's often far.

We in the Third Third are of the generation that set and understood the rules about cutting the "umbilical cord" so our offspring could grow up psychologically free. We didn't worry that "out-of-sight is out-of-mind."

My friend's attempts to placate me by showing the down side of family togetherness have failed. I think I'd change places if I could.

Meantime, I'll take solace in the adage, "Absence makes the heart grow fonder."

Watch It Kids,
We're Still In Charge

♦

There on the TV screen was Phil Donahue interviewing a teenage daughter who complained about her mother's unwillingness to help care for her new baby. Sy and Martha, in their Third Third, continue to work because they feel the burden to financially assist their 42-year-old son and his grown children. Their son criticizes that his parents never helped in other ways, and they accept the criticism, with apologies.

Ellen, my cousin, whose parents sent her to a finishing school, is an elegant woman, mother of two children. She cannot abide her father who appears uncouth now that she has the discernment of elite decorum.

Jim, a distant cousin turned red with embarrassment when his mother, unaccustomed to drinking a strong martini, became tipsy at an anniversary party.

Jean, a widow in the Third Third, tells that her daughter doesn't approve of her lifestyle: She should be slowing down, not traveling so much. Her daughter criticizes her dates.

Well, here come the judges! Is this a sign of our times?

When did the roles reverse? Is this another warning of the breakdown of our society, when the children become the rule setters for the parents?

Is our generation responsible for having broken the cycle of respect for elders? When we replaced the rod with books by Drs. Spock, Gissell and Ilg, did we spoil the system of leadership by the elders?

We certainly meant well. We, the parents of the Baby Boomers, were the first to raise our kids with vitamins, baby sitters and psychology.

We challenged the "Father knows best" adage and invented the theory that parents have to earn their children's respect. Dad became the pal at the ballpark and Mom left home for work or a PTA meeting or the bridge table. Neither wanted to be the disciplinarian, the "heavy".

We'll probably never know when or where the new trend of laissez faire in child rearing started. We can't tell now what was cause and what was effect. But there are signs that we post-war parents began to fear our children's displeasure and devoted ourselves to their comforts.

We limited our families so we could indulge the few offspring we had with all the material possessions we had ever wanted. Our children grew up feeling that the entire world owed them, especially their parents.

Perhaps this is a further demonstration that the progeny we spawned are slow to grow up. Part of the maturing process is that of growing up and away from parents while respecting them, even with their human foibles. Those who, after their teens, are still fighting their parents are more attached to childhood than they care to admit.

Throughout recorded and oral history parents set the rules and made judgments for the young, not the other way around. Elders, since human evolution began, have set the standards for society to live by. A role reversal would be revolutionary.

We can't demand respect, but with self-esteem we must call for respect for being in charge, for having the teaching role and responsibility.

We must retake the gauntlet of leadership and stand firm on the principles we've developed over our lifetime.

After all, kids didn't raise their parents and are therefore not responsible for their behavior. Children can change and divest themselves of most other relationships that don't suit them, but they can't get a new set of parents.

They're stuck with the parents who sired and birthed them. They might as well learn to tolerate us as we are.

Family Anger Is A Crippling, Needless Burden

♦

Terry looked bad, and when I asked her what was wrong, she hesitated. Later, over dinner, her husband David explained that a problem in their family has been eating away at Terry. It goes back many years.

It seems her 92-year-old father, who lives nearby, needs more attending now.

"But I'll defer to my sister, who was always his favorite. She's always short of money, and he gives it to her," Terry says. "Let my sister fly in to take care of him like I've done for years with no thanks."

Terry's anger seethed. She became white with rage as she told about years of disagreements with her sister. She doesn't like her sister's attitude, her demeanor, the way she talks to Terry, or her lack of responsibility. She is willing to give up the last moments of peace with her dying father to maintain her anger.

Nothing we could say would assuage her. She wears her wrath like a cloak.

David says this is better than the way it had been, festering within her. "At least now the anger is out where she can face it."

It didn't sound or look that good to us. Longstanding family disputes are a subject we hear about often in the Third Third. What causes people to bear such bitterness? Why would they carry the rancor for so many years?

We know four brothers who live in the same building, which their father built for them. Three don't speak to the fourth. This has gone on since the youngest married, and the grudge carries on now, to the third generation.

A friend hasn't spoken to her sister's husband for 30 years because her nephew, then 12, was rude to her. According to my friend, her brother-in-law didn't punish his son sufficiently.

The stories they tell of the genesis of their hurt are a justification and defense for their position. They tell their tales with righteous indignation. Sometimes the origins of the problem are blurred; only the anger remains.

The energy it takes to carry the resentment for so many years is debilitating. Like a seed between the teeth, the focus of everything is right there. Like a pebble in the shoe, they can't go forward until it has been removed.

Usually the problem is with a family member. It often has its base in sibling rivalry that dates from childhood.

The anger can cause physical damage to the adult who carries its heavy load. Depression can result from anger turned inward. To paraphrase author Wayne Dyer, unless you forgive the one you hate, dig two graves.

Women have traditionally been afraid to display anger. It was not considered ladylike to acknowledge conflict, particularly within the nuclear family. Thus we carried around small arguments until they reached family feud proportions. We released our feelings with sarcasm and biting remarks rather than by voilent outbursts.

To rid ourselves of the burden of bitterness, we must give vent to our emotions. If we don't, we pay a price that becomes more costly as we age. The Third Third is late enough to divest ourselves of embedded thorns.

We must pardon the one against whom we have a grievance and allow ourselves to heal. We must pardon the other after first we pardon ourselves. We must bury the hatchet.

Let's bring closure to ancient quarrels and residual anger. We must forgive and try to forget. We stand to gain as much as the person we're forgiving.

Pick up the phone and make peace.

Let's declare today Family Amnesty Day.

Things Change

Let Women Retire Too

◆

Among the snowbirds who dropped in on us during the holidays were friends who very methodically, very soberly, approached the prospect of retirement to South Florida.

They visited various neighborhoods, considered whether they wanted a large apartment or a small house, and noted where their friends clustered.

The one most important factor they had failed to consider was their real desire to retire. "Are you sure?" we asked.

Most men look forward to retirement; most women don't. This is probably because most men can't wait to leave the yoke they've carried all of their lives. Some men may even not have enjoyed their work.

On vacation here Vic finds the atmosphere dazzling. Last week he was shoveling his driveway to begin the long trek to work and a tension-filled day. Today, he played golf on a smooth green golf course, with four affable companions whose jokes he hadn't heard before. Last week he wore boots and layers of dark bulky clothes. Today he's dressed in a short sleeved light-colored shirt, plaid pants, and a casual sweater. He is being seduced by it all.

Fran, whose work has been at home, is aware that her job remains essentially the same in the south as in the north. Let's face it, a kitchen is a kitchen. She can't retire from domestic chores. And, though the media is filled with the promise of a new attitude toward his/her sharing household duties, few women in the Third Third of life today are in that kind of marriage.

Marketing, cooking, cleaning have been her responsibility for 40 years, and she knows she can't look forward to the traditional gold watch upon retirement. She will be giving up the cosy comforts of her home. She will be leaving her children, her neighbors, her favorite butcher and dentist for unknown surroundings.

I lunched with another friend, Irene, and three of her "in retirement" buddies who shared their world with me. They said it was hard to adjust at first. But the women, ultimately, seem to find a place. These four companions are an example. They play cards, lunch out, shop, and attend League of Women Voters' meetings.

"Although women's work is never done," says Irene, "We accept the inevitable and make the best of the bargain."

Men who worked intensely at a career usually don't develop hobbies or outside interests. This generation of retirees were yesterday's Depression youth who feel guilty if they play, even if they can afford to. "And how much playing can a grown man do?" asks one of the wives.

Men suffer in retirement from not having their own place in the sun. Whether he was a president of a company or a clerk, he had his own domain, a place to hang his hat, and now he has given that up. He's no longer boss over anything.

When our generation married, we started idealistically with a distribution of tasks. Men did the heavy work.

Women were left with only housecleaning, bedmaking, marketing, carrying children, and laundering which entailed toting twenty-pound loads of wet wash. The retiring couple again plans for equity in domestic maintenance.

He often helps to cut up the salad or to stop for a last minute supermarket pickup if the quick check-out lane is not too long. Meanwhile he becomes an authority on grocery shopping, offering critique about her not watching for bargains.

"I enjoy the four hours my husband is gone to his chess club twice a week," say one of the women. "He seems to have nothing to do with himself. He clings to me, wanting me for social contact."

"I've been his lifelong companion," adds another of the women. "I nurtured him and our children through every sore throat and toothache. I suffered with him when he lost his job, and all the other tribulations. I was the 'little woman'."

Their stories underscore the quip, "Behind every successful man there's a tired woman."

"Now in retirement, gimme a break." They all nod in agreement with Irene. "I married him for better or for worse. But not for lunch."

The Green Toothpick

♦

This is the story about a toothpick. It was a green toothpick and it broke the back of a 43-year marriage.

When Irene called to ask me to have lunch with her, I sensed an urgency in her voice. We have known each other since high school and have shared the hills and valleys of each other's lives.

"I'm leaving Hal," she announced while the hostess was finding a table for us. Never had the frequent, everyday bumps in their marriage brought her to so brash a decision. And she did seem to be decided. She wanted me to be a listener.

She and I had often discussed the term "love," and agreed that, although we felt a deep love for many people in different forms, we couldn't find an exact definition. Thus, my first question was rhetorical. "Don't you love him anymore?"

"Love has nothing to do with it," she was quick to answer. "He's retired and I'm tired."

Our generation of women moved from our father's home to our husband's home without ever finding out what we were capable of, or even what we wanted out of life. We were programmed to catch a man as soon as we could.

Our generation of men moved from their mother's care to their wife's care. He had a woman to care for him in his formative years, and traded her in for a wife who was expected to pick up the services his mother provided, plus a few more to sweeten the deal.

He feels righteous about deserving to play golf or tennis, read, putter in the garden, or take a part-time job that pays little but provides ego satisfaction. When he comes home to share his exhaustion, he expects dinner to be ready, either by his wife's hand or by a surrogate wife—a chef at a restaurant.

"My job," Irene moaned, "is to keep our physical, emotional and social life going.

"We sold the house and moved to a small apartment where, supposedly, my life of service would be lessened. But cleaning of our common facilities is unquestionably my responsibility. Remembering birthdays, providing gifts and other family connections is, of course, woman's work. Plans for social events, vacations, religious observances, travel, theater tickets all are my thing. He has the choice of going along or not."

A man over 60 feels no apology for conking out right after dinner. A man of that age can't be expected to care for another.

"Love has nothing to do with it. I've had it."

"But where will you go? What will you do?" I asked.

"At this age I can't expect to cultivate someone who will take care of me. I'll try to sell real estate and ask for a share of what we have saved together over the years. I can't take care of two any more. I just hope I can take care of one, me," she said.

Will she seek a divorce?

"This is a funny time," she explained. "If people can live

together without being married, we can try being married without living together." She seemed to have thought it through.

"I'll find a simple apartment where I can care for myself. I'll cook what I like. I'll eat what and when I want. I'll rest when I'm tired, and go for fun with people who want to be in my company.

"In 43 years of marriage, 52 weeks a year, doing laundry about twice a week, I've pleaded with him to not leave things in his pockets.

"Yesterday, when Hal was out watching a shuffleboard game, the washer ran over, flooded all over the kitchen and into the living room. The repair man, who finally came three hours later, said, 'You should not let such objects clog the machine.'

"When he pulled out the green toothpick I became very tired. Too tired to argue, or fight, or hope that I could be other than the caregiver of this marriage. So I'm leaving."

Gunning For Granny

◆

As we approach the entrance to K-Mart, I hold the door open for a family; an expectant mother, a pretty toddler girl, and a boy of about 8. "Such a nice family," I think, and become nostalgic for my own grandchildren, perhaps in some K-Mart far away.

"Nice family," I say to be saying something. The boy is already restless and Mama points to the toy section with, "Stop nagging, Scotty. Go play." He darts away. Mama moves to the clothing department and I start toward the garden supplies.

Somewhere between greeting cards and paper plates I hear "Bang, bang." There is Scotty, my new acquaintance, crouched at the end of the display case, aiming what looks like a submachine gun at me. He moves into a better position and, at a distance of about five feet, and with a businesslike grimace on his face, lets out a "rat-a-tat-tat" that causes me to lose my balance.

Not knowing what to do, I smile and say, "Be a nice little boy." He doesn't seem to hear or care. I move on my way, looking at a roll of gift-wrapping paper. As I place my selection into my cart and round the corner, I hear the blast of what, if I didn't already guess, is Scotty jumping heavily, a foot behind me, and audibly simulating a grenade. It was becoming a real encounter, a battle of wits. Could he get my attention by startling me? Or would I succeed in winning this nonverbal exchange by acting cool and not letting his demand for attention capture me?

Flashing into my memory were photos in history books, when I went to school, of Napoleon's troops on horseback, of the Civil War gray army shooting across a field at the blue army. Then there were the armies of World War I, firing from a distance at enemies they hadn't met and couldn't identify.

During my war, World War II, the still pictures in newspapers and magazines showed mostly nondirected shooting. The concept, at least to me, seemed to be to shoot, bomb, or otherwise destroy, but not to be personally involved in the act.

Since the advent of living room viewing of the combat in Korea and Vietnam, we've been shown the face of the soldier as he eyeballed his victim. Thanks to television, we were there as the youth aimed, fired, shot and killed his counterpart in the other camp.

Coming closer to our lives in time and space are the scenes, in our living room, of shootings on American streets, in homes, in shops, in schools. Recently we witnessed on screens only 10 feet from us the gory but real details of a South Florida customer shot in a restaurant, of a British vacationer bludgeoned to near death, of a couple who set a bomb in a Wyoming school. Scotty must have seen them, too.

Out of the corner of my eye, I see my assailant lurking behind the lamp display. I tell myself that I'm a mature adult, and I surely don't want to participate in this nonsense.

It's not my idea of fun and games. I move rapidly away from the ridiculous situation of entrapment by a mere child.

Is there a house detective or police officer I can call? And, if there is, what will I say that can explain my being intimidated by toy weapons? Would I not be the oddball in this day when real and fantasy shootings are so much a part of our entertainment?

He catches up to me, circumventing all other customers in his path, with nobody offering any resistance to this "terrorist" in our midst. No one even takes note.

"How about trading that gun in for a different toy that I'll buy for you?" I find myself offering to negotiate a truce in the fight in which I was unwillingly engaged. Scotty gets on one knee, takes a bead on my face, and lets out with a loud "Pow. You're dead!" He shouts this with a finality that renders me defeated.

I turn from him and rush out of the store, leaving behind the selections I had wanted to purchase. As I get into my car to drive away, I'm bewildered. He looked like such a nice little boy.

I feel the tears run down my cheek in memory of our civilization.

Whining Worker Speaks
Of Empty Dreams

♦

My high heels created a military beat as I clicked down the path leading to the office building. The man shuffling along in front of me turned, and in a stage whisper, muttered, "What's the rush?"

"I'm not rushing," I responded glibly as I passed him. "That's the way I usually walk." I had slowed to his pace, which seemed to be achieved by a conscious placement of one unwilling foot in front of the other.

"But it's only midweek. It's still 2½ days 'til 'Thank Goodness It's Friday' time," he argued.

It was a sultry May day. The air hung ominously, foreboding a steamy summer ahead. Were we two the fabled tortoise and the hare, each in our own style, avoiding exposure to the uncomfortable elements? No, it was more than mere physical comforts that our short dialogue had addressed. We had exchanged our diametrically opposing philosophical outlook about the days of our lives.

I was having a good day. We had accomplished the task

for which the volunteer board meeting had been called. I
then had lunch with a friend who worked across the street
from this building, in which I had an appointment at 2 p.m.
I looked forward eagerly to the rest of the day.

I had places to go and things to do, albeit self-created
business. By his attitude, he was essentially challenging
me and questioning my scurrying.

Was I being defensive of my lifestyle? And why not? I
was doing what I wanted to do. It's my life; I'm living it
my way. With this great freedom that grows every day into
the Third Third of life, my options expand. His seemed to
be narrowing.

The elevator was somewhere up in Otisland, or wherever
it is that they hide. I heard the scraping step of the plod-
der who arrived before the lift. As he joined me in waiting,
he picked up on our previous brief encounter.

"I'll be 65 this summer and can finally leave this situation after 18 years," he said in an attempt to involve me in
his life. He seemed to be asking for my tacit approval, my
understanding that he wanted to be finished.

But I didn't bite at his bait. Since turning 60, I've too often
been privy, in the company of contemporaries, to those
whining words of weariness.

"This August I'll be retired," he stated with pride that a
lifetime of pain was about to draw to a peaceful and blessed
conclusion.

I wondered what kind of torturous work he had suffered
through. Why had he felt so bound to the yoke that he
could not have changed his occupation, or at least his job?
Did he remain enslaved in support of the needs of a wife
and children and, if so, how sour the fruits of his labor
must taste.

No, I wouldn't indulge his self-pity by extending this conversation. I refused to be party by listening to stories about
years in the salt mines.

But I could no longer resist. He caught me with his promise of the answer to the question I'd been wanting to ask so many times: "Retire to what?" I ventured.

"Oh, I don't know." His voice had the same languid motion of his gait.

There was the elevator gaping open, and we entered, each headed for the fourth floor. We rode in silence for he had made the final, if listless declaration of independence from working, thinking, feeling, participating in the world in which he had lived for so many years. In a way, I wanted to know what would become of him in his empty dream of emptiness. But not enough to linger.

When the doors opened to free us from this short acquaintance, he slacked off to the right while I clacked to the corridor on the left.

I thought, "Thank Goodness It's Only Wednesday."

Nothing Is Forever

♦

T he dishes are certainly not the only thing I inherited from my mother. But it's so difficult to identify the feelings, the thoughts, the attitudes, the blessings. The longer I live, the more her positive impact on me grows.

Now I must come face to face with the inevitability of passing on and leaving something for my children. Somehow, it's easier to measure inheritances in terms of material objects.

Mayme, as my mother was affectionately called, was not a "things" person, except for her candlesticks and the set of flowered dishes.

Last week, when I had dinner guests, I was faced with a dilemma. There in my closet, taking up valuable space, was Mayme's china. When she died, I, the closest to her and her only daughter, took it. The china was her favorite possession.

Once, eight years ago, shortly after it became part of my household, I used the dishes. They certainly were pretty; the gold rim circling the cascade of flowers. But, when I took them out of the dishwasher for the first time, I noted that some of the gilt edging had been erased. Thus, they were returned to storage and the china remained there until my daughter and daughter-in-law were both present and I thought it the appropriate time to pass off the space-consuming bulk. Neither of them was interested; to them these were just another set of old-fashioned dishes. I defended the full dinner service as family heirlooms and told of the genesis of these objects d'art, but the young women remained unimpressed.

Growing up in the 1920s and the depression that followed, I remember parties and celebrations which, being the dish washer and drier of the family, I resented. We had "company" dishes, the partial set of which most matched and were unchipped. The "everyday" dishes were an accumulation of leftovers.

Those were times when most middle-class working people lived economically, spending for food, shelter, and clothing for kids when there was no hand-me-down that fit. A complete set of tableware was acquired by the fortunate as a wedding gift, and that was it.

But my Dad got a new job, the best he had ever had, in Herkimer, N.Y., where Mother met and was accepted into a group of society women who cared about decorative things. Each Wednesday they traveled along the Erie Canal road to Syracuse to "pick up some pieces." They would rummage among the seconds that the china factory there could not sell as first quality.

Mayme caught the bug. Within a few months she joined the other women in taking pride in her finds. Dish by dish, the matched set of service for 12, replete with teapot and other accessories, was collected and displayed in an open hutch cupboard purchased for that purpose.

Thereafter, until the day she died, Mayme cherished "The Set." Even when Dad lost his job and finances forced my parents to move into a smaller abode, parties continued. A wedding for an orphan cousin, a graduation, a new job, and, of course holidays, were causes for celebration. Out came "The Set."

Last week, when I was planning the dinner party, I deliberated. I decided to discuss it with Mayme: "Should I use The Set, and wash them by hand? Should I use them, place them in the automatic machine, risking the finish, and enjoy my company? Or should I let The Set sit on the shelf in hopes that my progeny will find a better solution?"

I could imagine her response quite clearly:

"Don't be a fool," she would have said. "These are only inanimate objects, beautiful though they are. Use them and enjoy." She explained to me all through that night that dishes are tools, a means toward a goal. The objective of having pretty things is to look and admire them in use, not in a static situation.

She would have been disappointed to learn that I still needed her advice at this age. I reminded myself of her lifelong message: Life is to live today.

"Sure, The Set will disintegrate," Mayme would have reminded me. "Nothing is forever."

The next evening when our guests admired the beautifully set table, I explained that the dishes had belonged to my mother. There was something festive that evening; an abandonment of worries about tomorrow. Our guests, all in the Third Third, were caught up in being lighthearted, and we agreed that life is short and the end is near and nothing is forever.

When my children review the earthly possessions I leave, they won't find a full, matched set of china. There won't really be much material for them to deliberate over.

I hope they will find this credo, this *joie de vivre* that Mayme left as her will and testament to me.

Thanks Mayme.

Holding Old
Habits In Check

♦

They both grabbed for the check. Arnie, 100 pounds heavier than she, prevailed.

He rose to his full macho sitting position as, I expect, most red-blooded American male chauvinists in their Third Third would.

He declared, like Moses giving the laws to the Israelites, "When a woman is with me, I pay the check."

Lillian, a friend I had made during my work with the Commission on the Status of Women, boldly argued. She prefaced her speech with an explanation that the position she takes now is a result of trial and error.

"I haven't got a special man to go out with. The demographics are such that women outlive men. There are about twice as many single women looking for a man at this age, than men looking for women of my age. As I grow older, the gap widens. So, I can't have too realistic expectations of changing that situation now or, perhaps, ever. I've adjusted to an acceptable way of life."

She, 14 years a widow, has thought through the situation.

She quotes from one dictionary that defines a widow as "a leftover." On checking my dictionary, I find a second meaning: "An extra hand or part of a hand of cards dealt face down and usually placed at the disposal of the highest bidder."

"Furthermore, we live in a society of couples. With all the changes that the women's movement has brought about, it's still a boy-girl world," she says impassionedly. "Other widows and divorcees sit at home or socialize only with other women. Although I enjoy the company of many women, I want also to be with my married friends."

Both Arnie and I agreed so far.

"Many married women are wary of the company of an 'extra'. The 'extra' becomes supernumerary, the fifth wheel of the wagon. It may be insecurity about the fidelity of the husband, or wanting to be the dominant female, or jealousy of the freedom of those unattached, or any number of other factors. Whatever, we in the single society often feel unwanted in the company of couples. It's as if Noah handed down the law of 'two-by-two'.

"When the man offers to pay the check, it is from the joint coffers. Understandably, the wife has a use for those dollars for needs of her own. And, really, I'm not hers or his responsibility. I work and I have my own money. I like their company and am very pleased when that can be accomplished."

She has risen to a pitch on a subject which, apparently, has been discussed many times.

Conversely, she posits, if she pays her own way, she can comfortably ask to be included in an evening out. Last week, she said, a party of nine went out for dinner and a show: three pairs and three single women. When the dinner bill arrived, one man divided it in ninths, and announced how much it pro-rated per person. Nice and easy.

I interject a thought that the single woman, wanting to

retain her friendship with couples, could initiate an invitation. "Why can't she make a party and be hostess by way of reciprocating?" I ask.

Arnie recalls an incident many years ago. Several times we invited Ginny, a former colleague of mine, to join us for an after-work meal. Each time she would offer to pay her way; each time Arnie refused to permit it.

She invited us to her home for dinner and Arnie felt ill-at-ease about the preparations she had made. She had unpacked and washed china she hadn't used since her divorce. Her three boys had been polishing silver and washing glassware all afternoon. We protested that she had gone to too much trouble, to which she answered, "Arnie made me do it. I have some pride too."

Later that night, as we drove home after helping to wash and put away the china, he said he understood the woman's position.

The dialogue continued between Arnie and Lillian at lunch. He said his ego is at stake. He said the man's taking charge of money matters is a custom that is carved into the history of our age group, etched in stone, and remains sacrosanct.

"So take the money," she pleaded. I thought she had prevailed, but just as Arnie was allowing logic to overcome him, he said, "I can't, yet."

Old habits die hard.

Women Need To Know Family Finances

♦

anking institutions are awesome, although they are today no match for the high-ceilinged, marble-columned, uniform-guarded edifices we in the Third Third remember from our youth. In depression, war and recovery periods, when we began our financial dealings, money was a very serious matter.

Over the years we have worked, saved and spent, and wished we could spend more. Yet, today there is an amount of security in knowing not only who and what we are, but how much we're worth in dollars. We must live with whatever we have accumulated, because we can't expect our earning capacity in the future to be what it was in the past. We can be comfortable with our financial status, rich or not.

We sat next to each other, the well-dressed, well-groomed woman about my age, waiting our turn at the savings and loan office. She fidgeted, rose to check where she was on the list, and said, "I'm always uneasy here." She went on to explain that her husband had died two years ago, and although he had left his affairs in order, they had been his affairs.

"After all, what do women know about money?" his voice still echoed.

When I was finally seated before the customer service representative who takes care of me on the few occasions when I can't do my business by mail, I asked if the reaction of that woman is usual.

"Are you kidding?" she responded, and went on to tell about the many widows whom she serves. "She may have no idea of her dollar worth. In this age group"—she lowers her eyes as if to apologize for the euphemism about older people—"money matters were taken over by the husband. The wife had her responsibilities and, especially if the man was a retiree and no longer had anything else that was his role, he clung to caring for the finances."

It's too bad that in addition to her grief at losing a lifelong companion, this woman is faced with the money matters so scary to her. You'd think that today, with the women's movement and all that it encompasses, things would have changed. You'd think she would have taken the time and trouble to learn what's going on.

All women who become widows panic to begin with. Some never get over the fear of ending their days in poverty. Some rise quickly to take over managing their money. Some begin to make changes in their investments, hoping to do better than their husbands did, and some actually do better. Many try to learn what finances are about, not making any immediate dramatic changes but moving to care for themselves. They begin to cope with paying bills on time and budgeting so they can have enough for the foreseeable future. Some blossom, enjoying their new power.

"For instance," the banking agent told me, "one woman I heard about recently almost sold her home immediately after losing her spouse because she didn't know how she would pay her insurance and other bills. After going over her bank books and records, she found she had almost $300,000, the interest from which could afford her an adequate life style." She was advised to get an accountant. Some widows are overwhelmed by the large numbers, mistakenly thinking they can live on their principal. They begin to spend wildly. The widow may go on a cruise and meet a dapper man who offers to take care of her and her financial burden, and she allows herself to be seduced.

The long lines at the tellers' windows are twice as long at the beginning of the month. Many people bring in their Social Security checks, not trusting the mail, wanting to see the deposit and the month's interest recorded in their book. They don't mind the tedious wait, sometimes over an hour long. They seem to feel a security in the touching, the feeling, the personal involvement in the process of the transaction.

The Depression left an impression on these people. Many tell memories of growing up without knowing if their father or, later, their husband, would be able to bring home a paycheck the next week. The money in the cookie jar was the defense between poverty and dignity. Worried and still carrying the scars of bygone days, they like to see their names on an account, large or small.

It must be a confusing situation for someone who has never handled substantial amounts of money. In the long run, we must all learn to take care of ourselves. Just having an account could give a reason to enjoy.

Rich or poor, it's good to have money. But why wait so long to learn about it?

Husband's Retirement
Can Rock The Love Boat

♦

When Arnie's coin laundry was for sale, I had an uneasy, queasy feeling, like *mal de mer.* Someone was rocking the boat. A change of life was coming.

A willing buyer had offered a good price to a willing seller, and my husband, at 70, retired from his daily routine. We entered the first day of the rest of our lives with doubts and trepidation.

During his hard-working years, there were many times he looked with envy on those who had an income other than that earned from the sweat of their brow. With a sigh of relief, he signed the papers and handed over the keys and tools of his trade.

But the old saying is true: "Be careful what you wish for. You may get it." Can Arnie handle the freedom to do anything in the world he wants? Can I?

We're both mindful of the adage, "I married you for better or for worse, but not for lunch."

First he took a deep breath, slept in, surveyed the lawn

and environs of our living quarters, swam and watched afternoon TV. He has reached the "pinochle" of success. He even volunteered to help, in limited amounts, around the house.

Pretty soon, he'll begin to choose from the other options available to him. He can get a part-time job using the many skills he has developed over the years. But we hear other men shun the responsibility of even a small job. Also, the pay is demeaning, and it would be depriving someone who really needs the income.

He could volunteer his time. The choices range from tutoring through the school system and listening to students to serving in a hospital or old age home. Community service groups would be happy to have him.

He may take an interest in public affairs and become involved in politics. He may take up photography or coin collecting. Friends are waiting to play cards or make a golf buddy of him.

Probably this old man could learn new tricks at the many universities, colleges, high schools and other institutions.

There is an abundance of activities out there in this leisure society. He could do a combination of each, or none of the above.

Fortunately, we have prepared what we think will be an adequate financial structure to permit us to live an acceptable life style. We'll dine on fruits of past labors.

Why am I so tremulous? This summer we plan to take extended trips to visit our children, stopping on the way to smell the roses and see the world we've missed before. But then what?

Arnie wants me to retire, too, to spend more time with him. That's where the shakes are coming from. I've worked, in one form or another, all of my adult life, and I enjoy it.

I'll retire from that work I enjoy the least, and that which is becoming burdensome. I intend to defy the notion that a woman's work is never done.

I'll find more time to spend with my husband by giving up vacuuming, changing beds, cleaning the refrigerator, sweeping the garage, and other domestic maintenance tasks. I'll relinquish the routine jobs to someone else. I'll yield to eating more prepared foods, in or out.

We'll have some long patient discussions, re-evaluations and redefinitions of what is woman's or man's work. We've made it over many hurdles in the 47 years we've been married, and we probably will make this transition as well.

Meantime, I'll take two Dramamine and wait to see what develops.

The Way We Are

A Good Marriage Is Not A Product; It's A Process

◆

The media are focusing on the quandary of young women whether to marry. I'm going to take advantage of the privilege that accrues to us Third Thirders to look back at the road where we've been, and where you're afraid of stepping. You seem to want to play now, pay later. Or never.

You're asking for a guarantee for what you'll get, and I'm here to state that you're not buying a product, therefore there's no warranty. You are embarking on a process; enjoy the trip, without insurance.

Career choice is an issue separate from wedlock; not mutually exclusive.

I don't know the advantages of singleness, but one can guess free is fun, especially since the advent of "the pill." About marriage, about one marriage, I can tell, and I'll guess it's written between the lines of every marriage contract.

You'll get to promise to love, honor, and cherish the handsomest, kindest, smartest man you've ever met; the perfect prince. He, in turn, has the perception that you are

97

beautiful, charming, and possessing of all the virtues. That's why you're merging.

You'll get a consumer of household services; cooked food, clean laundry, aspirin and stamps in endless supply for the asking, "where do we have more toothpicks?"

Don't plan on a training program. Research among my friends who have tried for decades leave us convinced that men are unteachable in mundane matters of supply and demand in the home.

You'll get someone who eats the chicken salad you had planned for tomorrow's lunch. But you'll get into a warm bed on a cold night.

You'll get a partner who forgets to tell you he lent most of your life savings to his deadbeat cousin. You'll get involved in heated dialogue, sometimes even arguments, that end in "you're as bad as your mother." But there'll be someone to go with to the hospital when a dear one is there.

You'll get to believe old wives tales that tell, "the way to a man's heart is through his stomach." You'll get patronized, especially in the company of others of his gender, about women's non-understanding of the stock market, foreign affairs, or environmental control. If you're lucky, you'll get acknowledged as a smart lady for running a household on two thirds of what it takes to live at the standard he wants.

You'll get to congratulate him on his impending fatherhood. To which he will probably reply, "Oh, no. Not now!" And before long you'll both be grinning smugly and asking, "Why not?" And then the adhesive starts to set with each miracle you jointly produce.

You'll get someone to listen to your frustrations and joys in exchange for hearing endlessly about his boss' incompetence. He'll get to the crossword puzzle first. He'll over tip the waitress not for good service but because her skirt is tight.

He'll come home with, "What's for dinner," and then,

maybe, think of kissing you "hello." He'll open the car door for Margie while your hairdo shrivels in the rain. But he'll be there every evening, even if only to fall asleep watching the football game.

You'll get to do your own thing although it's surely more difficult for the woman in a traditional marriage to act out her potential. But, getting there is half the fun, and the achievements are that much sweeter.

You get a return on your investment of time and patience and commitment if you come into the arrangement seeing him as macho as the Marlboro man and as proper as Papa, but knowing that he's only human. Oh, is he ever human. If we make it to October, it will be 45 years for Arnie and me.

You get to sit in front of the TV set in a comfort zone. In the room are photos of the children and grandchildren for whom we have both been links in the genetic chain and who, we trust, will pick up on what we missed.

There are no guarantees. You get to pay your life and take your chances.

First Third Logic

♦

Dear grandson:

You may remember my last visit when you took me to your room to show me your fossil collection, your drawings, your very favorite bird book, and the essay for which you had gotten a good grade in spite of your worrying so much the night before. You gave me your diary to read so I wouldn't be bored while you practised your cello, and then you complained about how rough it is on an eleven-year-old fella who has so many obligations to fulfill before he's ready to go outdoors.

Grandmothers tend to remember those moments.

That afternoon you looked at the heading of some columns I had brought to show your family, and, because you're into fractions these days, you questioned why I call my column The Third Third. In our 11 to 65 discussion, you came up with about the best definition of any I've heard since I gave birth to the term.

Using your newfound arithmetic skills, you determined that life expectancy for my generation is about

100

75. "Bless his sharp little mind," thought this proud grandmother.

You went on to compute and to conceptualize.

"The first third," you guessed, "is where I'm at. It's when you have to take it all in. You have to work so hard to read history and memorize poetry and make geography maps and practise music. It gets harder and harder until you graduate from college."

You got to feeling sorry for yourself as you foresaw the oppression in your life until you would reach the quarter century mark.

The second stage of life, you envisioned, is to work, work, work. Why work so hard, you asked, and decided you would not become part of that struggle. However, you agreed, temporarily, that gathering information and skills is a reasonable way to hedge against a future of hard labor.

You, from your own thoughts and in your own words, saw that the second third is the productive time, the time to give forth what was collected in the first third, and you look forward to that. You haven't decided whether to do that as a cartoonist or a zookeeper, but surely not as a cellist.

When you got to reasoning about the third third, your face lit up. "That's the time you can do anything or nothing!" That's the best time, you contemplated. "But when that time comes, I wouldn't do nothing. I would do what's fun and nobody could stop me."

You've got it, kid.

I concur that it's the free time of life. It's the period to accept who we are; whatever mark we've made on civilization. It's a time to learn to play chess or volunteer as a court watcher or play golf or take a trip to China or be a nuclear-freeze activist. Or be free to just watch the grass grow.

The only problem is which of the goodies to choose from the cornucopia of possibilities.

What an occasion for joy and laughter and celebration

of life. What an opportunity to achieve that stage of life of resting on laurels, becoming self indulgent, without obligation, without guilt.

"Then why are the older people so sad?" you asked. "Why are people afraid to say they are old?" A good question, my child, but a tough one.

I answered, as I always do, that it's a matter of perception. I believe that the alternative to growing old is sad, inevitable, but that death is reality. We've all gotta go someday, and, in the Third Third that day is close, closer, closest. Therefore we must number our days and bring joy to each one by heightened awareness.

"What if you live beyond, is there a fourth third?" you asked with your new-found mathematical insight.

We don't know about that. I only know that I have a possibility, and a fair probability, of vitality and challenge for the next 10 years. And I intend to enjoy, to the hilt, whatever months, days, hours and minutes are inscribed in the book of life for me. Some people beat the odds, but I'm not counting on that. Today's the day for me.

As your interest suddenly shifted to your friend who called to play soccer, you threw over your shoulder, "Everybody has to be some age. I'm glad I'm eleven."

Dear grandson. I'm pleased you're you, and you're eleven, and I entrust you to take my place in thinking through 'what's it all about?' You're my incalculable future.

As for today, I'm enjoying the Third Third.

Spending Habits Steeped In Memories Of '30s

♦

Karl could hardly wait for us to be seated before he blurted out, "I'm ordering the most expensive item on the menu, even if I don't like it."

That subject became the agenda for our foursome dinner. Said Karl, "If my daughter can call long distance at 4:45 p.m., prime time, weekday rates, to tell me that Joey made the little league team, why am I being so economical?"

Shirley, his wife, tried to calm him but he was inconsolable. "We're saving it for them, and they can't spend it fast enough," he said.

We of the gray-haired age group were born right after World War I, when the country's economy had not yet righted itself. Then boom — the crash of 1929 which precipitated the Depression. Even those of us whose fathers were able to maintain a livelihood for the family were conscious of the problems that abounded around us.

I remember, vividly, my mother inviting my friend Anne for dinner every Wednesday. After the fourth week, I

protested, but mother vetoed my objection, explaining that
Anne's large family didn't have enough to eat, so the least
I could do was to hush my mouth.

The '30s, when we were teens, were the days of bread
lines, dust bowls, works programs and the start of the
welfare state. There were men on street corners selling
apples. It left its imprint on us.

During our dinner, four of us talked for a while, almost
fondly, of memories of saving string (Who knows when
you'll need it?), the backs of letters (to hand in homework),
and sharing an orange four ways (to prevent rickets).

Shirley recalled how she hated her cousin Rose because
she got to wear the hand-me-down dresses before her.
Arnie, my husband, still stings with embarrassment about
being sent to the butcher to ask for soup bones for his non-
existent dog.

Even in more recent days, when we became more affluent, we are restrained by old frugal habits. Our offspring
accuse us of being skinflints because we drive a perfectly
good 8-year-old, "non-sexy" car. They ridicule our shorten-
ing the hem of an old skirt to modernize it. They would
have us become less inconspicuous consumers.

We still make soup from scratch because we know the
quality of the ingredients. We read books from the library
or wait for them to come out in paperback. We polish our
own fingernails and we don't buy in fast food markets.

Karl grimaces with, "Now my son pays 18 percent interest
charges on his credit cards because he forgets to send the
check on time."

I remember the pain in the purse when my grandchildren
were little and their parents would let them order liberally
at a restaurant, and then reject most of the meal.

Why did we work so assiduously, save so methodically,
to now deny ourselves luxuries when we can afford them?
For the children?

Perhaps not. Maybe we are locked into patterns of self-denial and rationalize the reasons we feel more comfortable with a larger bank balance than with a video cassette recorder. Could it be that we would, inwardly, like to take that trip around the world, but are guarding against the possibility, if not the probability, of becoming dependent on our children for payment of large hospital bills or for care in our old-age? Is it, indeed, the fear of living too long with too short resources?

Are we tight-fisted because we're not up with the times in knowing what latest fad or label is hot and what's not, and couldn't care less?

By the time we've accumulated enough assets to be free spenders, if our conscience would allow, we no longer need or desire the things money can buy. As Karl drained his glass of wine, to make his Chateaubriand, fried onions, and creamed vegetables more palatable, he patted his mid-section and said, "At this age, I couldn't, and shouldn't, eat this way too often." We all agreed.

When you see the bumper sticker, "I'm spending my children's inheritance," you can believe it or not.

Doctors' Ills Kill
Faith Of Patients

◆

Dorothy, the doctor says you have to come in two hours earlier," she virtually shouted into the phone. "That's the way it is."

The young woman in white impatiently tapped her long, red fingernails. "Sorry. You'll just have to find a ride."

She looked to me for understanding about the rough times patients give the busy business staff in the medical office. The waiting room was full of people in the Third Third.

When she turned to me to say, "That will be $150, Claire," she lost any empathy I might have had. The price had been established on the phone when I made the appointment to see "The Big Man, The Specialist."

How could I protest the high price when the doctor has to pay such high malpractice insurance premiums, and when Medicare would reimburse me for part of it?

He turned out to be an arrogant pipsqueak, accustomed to being in command of aggressive young women who run his office officiously, and of older women who need his services and pay big bucks. I expected my check to be rung up on a cash register.

My visit to the doctor proved counterproductive. As I waited and waited, the only one aware that my time also has value, I pondered the deterioration of medical services in this richest of countries, and the physicians' flap about malpractice insurance.

Fixed in the minds of most of my contemporaries is the doctor whom Norman Rockwell immortalized on the Saturday Evening Post covers, depicting him as a healer. How else?

The doctor was the bright young man who at age nine took in any injured animal and dreamed of the day when he could treat ailing humans. His dedication earned our admiration, awe, respect and love.

"We'll ask the doctor." That meant things were serious enough to get an authoritative opinion. "The doctor said," was the final word of any argument. The caduceus was a symbol as holy as any religious icon.

Over the years, some doctors have assumed a position of power accruing only to those in a monopoly. Perhaps we, in our ludicrous ambition to stay alive forever, have granted them that power. How much further can they control the public's health without a revolt? There's got to be a comeuppance. Are they leading us and themselves, at long last, to socialized medicine in behalf of the public interest?

For many years, fostered by the GI Bill designed to help the returning World War II veterans be absorbed into the peacetime economy, government subsidized students and medical schools. Hospitals were overbuilt in the 1970s through federal monies. Socialization and public money for medical providers burgeoned and were gladly accepted by the medical profession.

Anyone who wanted to spend three years in study could get a loan that could be paid off in three years. What a great business investment. No wonder the competition was so keen.

The American Medical Association lobby has long publicly bad-mouthed controlled delivery of medical services. Of course.

Repeated studies and personal empirical observation show that people in countries where the government controls medical service have much higher quality and more affordable care. Granted, there are boondoggles in any bureaucracy, and there might be here if government control over delivery of medical services was instituted in the United States. But the public would be assured of the inalienable right to health care. What have we now to protect the many who aren't insured?

We in the Third Third, in ever-increasing need of medical care, are acutely aware of our dependence on doctors. When they strike, or euphemistically "withdraw services," we suffer as a group as much as or more than others. They control our fate.

Doctors, who now decry having to deal with insurance companies to protect their source of income, were the first to introduce and give support to third-party insurance companies who would assure them of payment by patients. Now that the shoe is on the other foot, it pinches and they're crying foul.

Couldn't we lessen the need for malpractice insurance by lessening malpractice? If, as they claim, it's only a small percentage of physicians who create the problem, instead of protecting each other by insurance coverage, wouldn't they do better to weed out those few?

The bell tolls for medical care left in the hands of greedy doctors. They've abused the privilege of power. It's time for government to protect us. One way or the other, we're paying for it.

Harry's Retirement Haven

◆

Plastic or paper bags?" he asks in the husky, deliberate voice of one who has asked the same question many times today. He moves methodically to arrange the bottles at the bottom, carefully layering the bread and other light-weight purchases on top.

He scans the platform as the checker rings and pushes my purchases forward. He gives thought to what he is doing, and does it well. He is a professional.

But I'm feeling uncomfortable. Here is a man, obviously deeper into his Third Third than I am at 66. Here is a man who does his job effectively and with dispatch, even though his body seems so frail. His shirt hangs out the back from the uniform apron and his baseball cap sits jauntily to one side.

I want to take over for him. I can pack my own groceries. I am not to the manor born. I don't need this man, so much my senior, to be waiting on me. And I mildly protest.

He looks at me with a mixture of disdain and pity: disdain for interfering in the operation of his business, and pity for my not understanding the way of the world. I yield. I pay my bill, presenting bonus stamps, and finish my negotiations with the cashier. Still, he is not ready to roll. He seems to be prolonging the chore of packaging to tease my restlessness.

I tell myself to calm down. I'm tired from a hard day's work. It's hot. Perhaps it's time for me to hang up the old typewriter. Maybe I'm getting cranky and crotchety. The easy life of Social Security beckons and I'm smiling responsively. The siren rocking chair creaks its whining song like a Lorelei seducing me to sit.

Finally he's ready to move out. He leads and signals me to follow with a flick of his head, like Fred Astaire's silent indication to Ginger, "Wanna Dance?" We head for the mammoth parking lot to find my hiding car.

"Looks like rain," is his opening gambit. I pick up the attempt at trivial conversation for the time that we will be together.

"Have you been working here for long?" I ask.

"Not as long as I hope to be," he answers tartly. "I hope they carry me away from here. And I hope I don't know it then."

Remembering the prevailing ethic of his youth and mine—"He who does not work does not eat"—I feel compassion for this old man who must carry these heavy loads of food for others so he can eke out a meager living. I'm already digging in my purse for the (disallowed) tip I will hand this man. He is quick to dispel any such thoughts.

"I don't work because I *have* to," he says, with a twinkle in his eyes. "I work because I have to—for myself."

His name is Harry. "If you're gonna write about me, tell them old geezers that old Harry likes to work."

Harry is a railroad pensioner. The $125 a week he nets from his job as a supermarket bag man is just pin money with which he takes his wife out to dinner once a week and buys the grandchildren tickets to come visit.

When Harry retired from the trains in Buffalo, he and the missus traveled quite a bit. No, I hadn't known that they got to go places for "next to nothing" as a family. They saw the Rockies and the Grand Canyon and went south to visit Harry's sister.

But each year, shoveling the snow became harder and harder. He got his warning like a loud clap of thunder. After the heart attack, he took his doctor's advice and moved to Florida.

Harry and his wife took on the responsibility of managing an apartment house. He said it was all right, but you were like a slave to all the tenants. "Harry, the walk needs sweeping." "Harry, would you bring in the garbage cans?" "Harry, when is the mailman coming?" It wasn't difficult, but it was aggravating. A person has to have some dignity.

After that he sat around watching TV, he took long naps, and he wandered around the mall. He became fat. He quarreled with his wife.

Some people at that age find a place on the golf course, or a place to watch the stock quotes, or a seat at a card table. Not Harry.

He got this job and for the past year and a half he has gotten up four mornings a week, gone to the store, punched in, done his work, punched out and felt good.

A person's got to have a place to go, and something to do.

The Best Surprise
Is No Surprise

♦

This particular morning Arnie went out, as he does every morning while I make the bed, to bring in *The Herald*. He came back looking dejected.

"The paper's not there!" he announced, as if he were telling me about an earthquake he had read about in a headline.

"It's no tragedy," I said with bravado and an attempt at humor. "We've faced and overcome adversities before, and we'll get by today."

In the Third Third, people are set in their ways, and have formed behavior patterns that are, shall we admit it, rigid. Little changes are hard to cope with. When we didn't get our paper, we moped around all morning, feeling disappointed, disrupted, disgruntled.

We tried the TV and caught Bryant Gumbel playing cat and mouse with then Vice President George Bush when I wanted to know just what his involvement had been in the Iran-Contra scandal. It was not enough.

I needed my morning fix of what had happened locally

and what was said on the editorial page. Arnie was missing the front section and the crossword puzzle. We were out of sorts, out of control.

When my car was in for repairs a few weeks earlier, I felt the same restlessness. Not that I particularly needed to go someplace, but that week I suffered from the feeling of confinement. Turning down an offer to use someone else's car, I stoically decided to take the bus. But after trying to find out about routes and schedules, I gave up that idea, then fought and won an inner struggle to prove myself adaptable. I took a book to the park and spent the afternoon in lovely weather, suffering all the while.

Joyce told of feeling discomfiture because her daughter hadn't called at 10 a.m. as she does each Sunday. Joyce paced up and down, worried, inconsolable all day, especially when her attempts to reach her daughter failed.

When the call finally came that evening, her daughter explained she had had an emergency at work and had left the house too early to call. Joyce described being tired and discombobulated, and ashamed of her seeming inability to cope with slight change.

Those are minor modifications in our daily lives. But when our dishwasher suddenly stopped dead in its tracks, it became a serious problem in our home, especially when it happened the week we were expecting company.

"Woe is me," I felt like crying, but was too ashamed that such a mishap could affect me. What did we do before these mechanical aids were so much a part of our lives?

How do people in other cultures manage? Surely they develop patterns of behavior that, if disturbed or broken, will disturb their equilibrium. I recall observing older women washing clothes on rocks at rivers in Switzerland, China and Poland. What if it rains, or someone else does her wash at one of the women's favorite rocks?

It is, indeed, a matter of being out of control. Those of

us who make it anywhere in the world, are those who can roll with the punches, weather the storm, rise above the temporary discomfort. How did I come through three years of waiting for World War II to end, believing every day would be the last? How did people involved in wars actually live through the interruption that bombings cause?

Is this a permanent condition, being so far into the Third Third that no change is possible?

Courageously, stout-heartedly, with stiff upper lip, I'll try to face my day as an adaptable, mature person who can put things into proper perspective. Arnie called the circulation department and they said they would bring a replacement paper right to our door.

"Tell them it better not happen again," he said as he left early to go on his appointed rounds.

Rather than try to do something constructive, I ran away from reality. I went to the beach and bought a paper on the way. Arnie bought one too. But it wasn't the same as reading it first thing in the morning.

Widowed Loners
Need Not Be Lonely

♦

We Americans are gregarious people, often insecure in solitude, and unsure and uncomfortable with ourselves when alone. It could be a learned behavior; we're taught that loners are unhappy or unwanted people. Alone does not have to mean lonely. Alone is a physical state; loneliness is a condition of the mind.

Who set up the Kingdom of Coupledom? Who said that forever more we must travel in pairs? It may have been necessary for Noah's animals, for procreation of their species, but it isn't necessarily so for my peers in the Third Third.

Unfortunately, many men in our culture leave this good earth before women. Fewer than four of ten people older than 65 live with a spouse, according to *American Demographics* magazine, leaving many of us without a mate, possibly for the rest of our lives. Statistically, as of 1987, including widows and divorcees, women will spend only 43 percent of their lives living with a husband.

My friend Jean speaks for Third Third singles angry at

fate. An attractive, sparkly woman who was married for 42 years, she desperately declares, "Most of me died when he did. I can't go on living alone." As a young woman, she moved from her father's home to her husband's and had never in her 64 years lived alone for any length of time. She feels she needs a man to validate her, to assure her that she's OK.

Those of us in long-term marriages cannot argue with that. But, when fate rules arbitrary singlehood, it would seem a self-punishment not to try to create a new lifestyle.

With the projection that most women in their Third Third will face this dilemma, it behooves us to crack the negative image of aloneness. To have loved our husbands does not mean we can't enjoy the later years without them.

Accepting this can bring twenty or more years of relaxation and the contentment of enjoying our own company. The unhindered delight of doing exactly what you want to do and when you want to do it can prove to be among life's peak points.

A phone call from another friend, Edith, brought us together for dinner for the first time in a couple of years. Over cocktails, she told of her climb out of the dark pit of loneliness and despair.

For two years after she had been widowed, Edith went into seclusion and isolation, licking her wounds from the blow. This year, she's talking about a part-time job, trying new foods and joining a yoga class. With a youthful glint in her eye, she says: "I've suddenly become interested in foreign films. Between viewing the movies and meeting with the society and its activities, my time is so filled I have to make a special effort to keep in touch with old friends I value."

She's finding dignity in her independence and freedom; a new energy in retrieving buried interests. She has self-reliance in venturing forth to meet new people and new experiences. "Once I decided to give up my anger that was isolating me and my jealousy of those whose lives go on uninterrupted, I find each day exciting. It's a test of loyalty to myself to select from choices of what to do today alone, or with a person whom I pick to spend my time.

"It's scary at first," this seemingly shy, fragile-looking lady says. "It took a lot of gumption to begin to see myself as a meaningful, important and complete person. But it was worth the effort."

She proceeded to tell me about her long-range plans to travel in this country and abroad and her crowded calendar of local social activities.

"You just have to learn what you want to do alone and what you want to do together with another. You have to make plans for something to look forward to whether it's going for an ice cream cone or to Australia."

Then you reach out to touch someone.

I'm pleased that Edith chose me to spend her limited time with. When life handed her lemons, she made frozen daiquiris.

Sweet
Righteous Indignation

♦

After the leisurely morning ablutions, watching the TV chatter and thoroughly reading the newspaper, I smugly meandered out early, allowing for the exigency of impacted traffic.

I was prepared, calm and ready, to meet the audience that was waiting to hear my pearls of wisdom.

In my Third Third, I've a conscious desire to take the pressure out of my life by planning ahead to avoid tension and strain. Raising the garage door, I saw Fred's car parked so it blocked both our cars. Arnie and Fred were mindlessly bicycling to some distant destination, leaving me trapped.

"Be calm," I said to myself. After all, I'm a mature woman. I can't allow myself to get bent out of shape by such a small incident. "Keep your cool."

I could feel the beat in my heart like the unrelenting beep of a phone left off the hook. My palms felt like limp sponges. My head was like a dropped clock with parts jumbled and the alarm screeching.

Fortunately, the day before, during a major overhaul at

the beauty salon, I had thumbed through a plethora of magazines. Most had an article on coping with stress. What a blessed portent.

As I tapped the lessons learned from these self-help publications, I felt some steam ooze out of my boiling body, like turning the soup down from high cook to simmer.

One article had suggested meditation as a relief from stress. With hands folded in my lap, breathing deeply, I started to repeat "one, one, one," but rather than lessening, my blood pressure was growing like yeast cake on a warm stove.

Another guru had recommended "imaging", picturing the up and down of a dilemma. The best could be for a friend to come by to visit and drive me. The worst would be that I not keep my commitment and my name, held pristine for many years, would instantly become mud.

Self-hypnosis was another method touted for achieving equilibrium. I sat before the lamp-pull, which, when I'm trying to call up brilliant prose, has a mesmerizing effect. It was not a potent weapon against this intense angst.

After using a suggestion that I snap a rubber band or pull on an earring, it felt so good when I desisted that I was able to think along more pragmatic lines. I reviewed my options.

A cab from here to there would probably cost $25, if it would get here and there before the event was scheduled to close. Calling a friend was also impractical; those who lived near were working. I could desecrate Fred's car. I could cry.

Or I could inch out of the garage at an angle to avoid his car on a route over our newly planted shrubs. Deciding to make the value judgment of a mature woman, I mowed down the plants and made my way into the traffic.

Even en route, the tension didn't abate.

One magazine writer who is a psychologist said that if I took a mental picture of the negative situation, reduced it in my mind's eye to the size of a postage stamp, pasted it on an imaginary envelope and mailed it to the tooth fairy, or whomever, I would be forever rid of the fury churning inside me.

Later, on the return trip, I was still stewing.

Finally, home at last, I confronted Arnie.

"How could you do that to me?" I blurted out. "Do you realize how you ruined my day?"

Suddenly, like milk spilling from a dropped bottle onto my new dress, the rage poured out. Also, I had a revelation gained from so many years of living, including 48 years of marriage.

Intelligent women follow the advice of experts, but in the long haul, nothing relieves tension like righteous indignation. Nothing makes you feel better than to have a husband—or someone else close by—to blame.

It's Not So Easy

Fair Weather Friends

♦

I f you notice two women past the bloom of athletic youth playing on one of the many tennis courts in West Broward, don't presume they are enjoying themselves.

Six years ago my friend Fonda and I were having our lunch at the usual greasy-spoon diner, complaining that we're getting pudgy from sitting at a desk all day. We both acknowledged that, at our advanced age, the tendency to bulge would be irreversible.

Unless we exercised.

"Let's play tennis," she said on the memorable day we have come to rue. She, in retrospect, blames me for initiating the idea.

Although she is my junior by many years, she tends to have lapses of memory. Because we are friends, I overlook these. I know she is responsible for our foray onto the court every weekend at 7:30 a.m. In case some of you have never been out at that time, let me assure you, it is very early.

We grew up in the post-Victorian era when mothers' sole ambition was to turn out well-bred young ladies. And young ladies in those far gone times didn't play ball. Thus, when we lined up with 18 others at the Nova-Davie adult school for a tennis clinic, we quickly noted that we belonged in the sub-beginner class. Our sports acumen has remained equally matched since then.

Three semesters later we ventured onto public courts, where we were embarrassed as each rally ended with the ball three courts away. Part of our problem was that we wore old shorts and shirts in contrast to the well-groomed players surrounding us.

"We have to dress for success," we agreed.

The following week we became fashion plates of the court. In spiffy tennis dresses with pom-poms properly overhanging Nike shoes, we felt we were on our way to Wimbledon. But not yet.

We had ordinary rackets. Our husbands, impressed with the persistence of our athletic dedication and wanting to encourage our quest for well-being, provided birthday presents of suitable quality. With that investment, we were committed to continue. We had, as it were, a tennis tiger by the tail.

Dressed to the nines with our first-class gear of color-coordinated headbands, water buckets and tote bags, we made our move to Plantation Center courts. The lively new ball, meeting the tense new racket, ricocheted over the net, over the fence—a home run into the canal, setting egrets to wing.

We then graduated to a single, more private court. But, Chrissy Evert, fear not.

Now we play regularly every weekend morning that is dry. After all, it would be counterproductive to our health to chance slipping on the wet ground.

However, we are prepared for residual puddles from Broward midnight showers with a (color coordinated) broom tucked into the trunk of the car. I'm getting tired, though, of my husband's corny remark that if I run out of gas I can always ride home on the broom. That's the down side of a 44-year marriage.

Heat is another story. We must reckon with the equation of sun-plus-age-plus-stamina and come to the quotient of 17½ minutes for ball in play. Don't laugh. The sun becomes more direct and more oppressive every minute that the day moves toward noon. That's not for a 64-year-old woman who stifles complaints about thirst, arthritis, sleeplessness and weak ankles.

So the rule between us is that we hit balls to our own modified International Tennis rules, which we would be hard put to explain to any challenger. We play for as long as 20 minutes and then we rest. Ah, welcome recess.

A drink of water, a wipe of the cloudy eye glasses, an exchange of platitudes about politics and the weather of the past week, and then we really get into it. The gossip. Did her son get a raise? Yes, I had a call from my children. Did her daughter's new beau prove as worthwhile as anticipated? So goes a half-hour and the Florida sun sends its oppressive message: "Come back to the court."

We do, reluctantly.

That's our usual Saturday or Sunday fun in the sun. We feel healthful, purified, ready to accept our bodies as support for that valued computer, our brain.

This morning the alarm went off at 7 a.m. and, thankfully, I saw raindrops.

Driver's Responsibility – Knowing When To Stop

♦

I t's never pleasant to visit someone in the hospital. But
I was particularly upset by the visit to Fred. He and his
wife were relieved that as serious an automobile
accident as Fred had been involved in, he had sustained
only cuts and bruises to his body and face. "Thank
goodness. It could have been worse."

Sharing the room was a 19-year-old fellow in traction,
swathed in bandages. He had just come off the critical list.
I overheard his mother saying, "Thank goodness. It could
have been worse."

The two roommates, there as a consequence of separate
accidents, seemed to be set up as antagonists and we, the
onlookers, the societal victims they are out to get.

Both told about the events, explaining it was the other
guy's fault, as if it mattered. Both were victimized by their
own abuse of the driver's license. Fred's vision is impaired
by age; the young man had a few beers too many.

Recently, I felt anxiety about my 16-year-old granddaughter driving in Ohio. Would she become a statistic

among the large number of under 25-year-olds? Although this group is the target of concern by insurance companies, police and families, I consoled myself, realizing that the young have youth on their side—bright eyes, sharp hearing, alertness and quick response time render them potentially good drivers.

The other group of drivers causing concern is those older than 60. Although the wisdom of experience is ours, the body deteriorates and the eyes, ears, alertness and reflexes start to corrode. Most are careful, and therefore good drivers. Age is not really the determinant as much as responsibility.

Yet, visiting Fred I felt ashamed, for the last time I was in his car, he was driving down the center lane, made a left-turn signal, and turned right. Brakes screeched all around us, but nobody talked about it so we wouldn't embarrass him.

Afterward, I asked Lil why, if he can't see, does he continue to drive? "His ego is involved," she explained. "He would feel worthless if he couldn't drive."

Bending the rules and winking at reality is not trustworthy behavior. Fred had not passed the eye exam in Florida (the test that is so outrageously easy it cries to be revised). But, at the time of the accident, he had a valid license that had been renewed by mail from New Jersey—without testing. The young man, we learned, was driving while his license had been suspended, so he faces criminal charges. But he's hoping for a good lawyer and a lenient judge.

We were shocked to hear about the 81-year-old woman who had a current driver's license despite a history of numerous accidents. She drove onto the sidewalk, killing three people. This week we learned about a 20-year-old who, while drunk, killed two people. He was sent to jail for 17 years. How long he is off the streets now is not as significant as the fact that he had seven previous suspensions. He was telling us something. Why wasn't anybody listening?

We, the potential losers in the community, wanting to cut back the horrible record of American fatalities on our roads, must call for more responsibility from each of us who takes the wheel in hand. If we can't self-regulate, we need more stringent laws and more frequent testing for all ages, particularly those with a history of accidents.

Sensible seniors, let's be maturely realistic and move into another stage of life. It could have its compensations. We can avoid automobile maintenance and parking problems. We can sit back and leisurely leave the driving to someone else. The cost is less than maintaining a private vehicle.

Let's take charge of ourselves, and of others on whom we have influence, before it becomes much, much worse.

The lives we save will probably be our own.

Too Much Of
A Good Thing

♦

How could I resist a "perfect day" at the Spa? The enthusiastic invitation promised that the health and fitness facilities and staff of this world-class luxury resort could make a difference in just one day.

Fitness this 64-year-old body sure could use. But I was a little concerned about changes that would be too drastic. After all, it has taken me so many years to get used to this body, and my husband accepts me as I am.

Curiosity about what goes on behind the walls of such a place made me submit myself to the seemingly impossible task they had undertaken. I came willingly, and they sure tried.

After an introductory tour of the posh facility I was given a "theme" burgundy uniform, and started on my personally-designed program.

My imagination was piqued by the title of the first activity, "coed stretch." This turned out to be a gym full of men and women, guided by a jock, limbering up in preparation for the strenuous metal monsters on which they would work out. Next door, women were prancing around to the urgent aerobic rhythm of a female jock (a jockey?) Part of the implied promise of the "perfect day" was that I might find myself engaged in locker room talk with such notables as Linda Evans, Zsa Zsa Gabor or Martina Navratilova. I settled for chitchat with a couple of local sisters I knew, who had come to spend the day with each other away from daily routine. Among others were two business-women from New Jersey, a new widow, a new divorcee, a new bride whose groom was doing his routine on the other side, and a 78-year-old who was taking the activities a little slower than her daughter and granddaughter with whom she came.

They came for a day or an extended stay. Some are spa-hoppers who travel over the country. "As women move in-to the business world, we need to strengthen our bodies," said one, whose body didn't need much improvement by my standards.

Lunch, which had been touted as "elegant and nutri-tionally serious," was not hearty, but adequate. The adjec-tive that came to mind was virtuous.

In one day, I voluntarily crowded a variety of body in-dulgences befitting an ancient Greek goddess.

The body massage, a "shiatsu pressure point" method, felt good as the first of many handlings this body was to go through. The facial, executed by the "esthetician" was a process of putting on, rubbing in and taking off a series of balms, potions and creams.

The hot herbal wrap was achieved by encasement in several layers of steaming hot towels that were soaked in some concoction, and then enclosed by rubber blankets. Cold applications to my forehead and neck jolted me out of what could have been a welcome nap.

The loofah treatment consisted of an attendant coming menacingly to hose me down, then salt me down, then rub the entire body down with a sponge mitt. Rotating this procedure is called "exfoliation." I abstained from the offerings of pool aquacizes and nude sunbathing discreetly hidden from view.

But I did allow myself into "hydrotherapeutics." In the plunge pool I felt like a Roman princess. After the Swiss shower—17 shower heads beating water from 17 angles, automatically changing temperature from ice cold to boiling—I felt, simply, washed out. The Finnish sauna offered no alternative to sitting on a hot wooden bench while feeling very finished. The Turkish steam bath completed the process of melting me down. I was rendered pliable.

Had I come here by choice?

I was patted, primped, painted, pulsated, plunged and pampered. And what's more, I was pushed, flushed and gushed. I was salted, steamed, showered, scraped and sprinkled. That's not all. I was massaged, mangled and manipulated.

Finally, the parts that show the most were attended. In the hair and beauty salon an artist applied to my face neutralizer, foundation, eye liners, under-eye cover, mascara, blush and highlight, not necessarily in that order. Whatever weight had been rubbed off my body earlier was put on my face. But I looked as glamorous as this lax, though polished, skin could look.

I felt fit. Fit for my own dear bed.

Enjoy as I did, I don't know how to evaluate it. Arnie did recognize me.

Biopsy Offers Reprieve

◆

I shook for three days, and didn't tell anyone my secret. It was too horrible to discuss.

Now I sit in the doctor's office waiting for her to call me in to review her findings. On a recent visit, she sent me for tests. The results arrived, and I was invited back to discuss them. The physician had mentioned, in passing, that perhaps it would be wise to take a biopsy. I'm trembling. I'm scared.

The work "biopsy" rolls off the tongue of health professionals very easily. Those of us who have little medical knowledge find that a buzz word. Biopsy is a flag euphemism for "we suspect that you may have cancer." The word packs a wallop!

So here I am, about to become one of the club of almost a million Americans who, this year, are expected to be, unhappily, in the membership.

Sitting there waiting for further instructions from the M.D., thoughts, ugly thoughts, impose themselves. "Be still my heart." I try to calm myself with reason and knowledge that only a small percentage of those who fear the big "C" actually are victims. I look toward the door with an eye to an escape route, but know there's no escape. I also know that we, over 50, are the most vulnerable, and that early detection is the best safeguard.

I should have spent more time reading to my children (who now are parents). I should have taken vitamins more regularly. I could have allowed my husband to have the last word once in a while. I might have kept my house a little cleaner. Too late.

I speculate on what the doctor has in store for me. Will she say that the disease can easily be eliminated with a slit and a cut and, after surgery, I'll be as good as new? Or does she have in store for me that evidence of abnormal cells are there, confirmed by the definitive test, a biopsy?

Forward in my consciousness are three brave women friends. My stockbroker announced last year that she was going in for "exploratory" surgery. There was nothing to be concerned about, she assured me. A call to her three days later revealed that she lost a breast, but she was delighted at that small sacrifice in exchange for a tentative assurance of good health. She's planning a trip to the Vancouver fair with two of her granddaughters.

A schoolteacher friend, whom I haven't seen for a while, told me last summer she had cancer surgery, and that it was rough. She described the emotional impact as 20 million megavolts, as she faced death daily until her body went into remission. She tells, though, about her family's reaction. "For the first time in my life I'm getting TLC. Tender loving care has always been my forte, my role to give. Now, suddenly, I'm on the receiving end. Now I feel good, and it's great."

My friend, who denies that she has the kind of cancer that could be fatal, is the one who is really maximizing this new phase of her life. She denies that she is at the edge of life. "The worst that can happen is that I find I'm going to die soon, so I might as well live while I can," she cooly explains. "The best outcome can be that this is all a bad dream, and that I'm fine," she reasons. "So surely I should go on living fully and the best that I can."

I'm back to brooding. What would the terminal stage be like...Would I be in excruciating pain, or do they prescribe palliatives? What would I want to take care of as a final gesture? Should I dust my books and straighten my lingerie drawer? Whom would I want to see and be with at the end? My children and grandchildren. Why don't I plan a visit even if it's not the last time?

The doctor calls me in. She says I'm OK. She assures me that someday I'll die. But not right now.

She gives me a reprieve. I thankfully accept this gift of more time for loving more people, reading more books and enjoying more pleasures. The world stretches out before me like a cornucopia of goodies from which I can choose.

I've faced mortality and come back.

I'm one of the lucky ones. But will I remember to live smart?

Exercise: Painful
Precaution Against Aging

◆

According to the actuarial tables, I can expect to live to be 90.

The threat of incapacitated old age with creaky bones, infirmities and other results of stagnation looms as a frightening situation to be avoided at all costs. What does one in the Third Third do to stave off the crippling effects of aging for as long as possible?

"Exercise!" the pundits advise.

Easy for them to say. Faceless bylines in the press, probably in their 20s with firm, vital, animated bodies. Granted, Jane Fonda and Raquel Welch seem to be successfully pushing away the outward signs of aging. Is their retention of youthful face and torso attributable only to their vigorous fitness programs? Please someone, tell me otherwise.

Wanting to take advantage of the odds available to me, I decided seven years ago to take up tennis—my partner is fifteen years my junior. Neither of us had played ball before and we approached the challenge with enthusiasm and a pact that we would motivate each other to move our bodies.

We duly took lessons, bought the appropriate equip-
ment—rackets, dresses, drink buckets and dual-colored
balls—and we agreed to play every day that we didn't have
to work.

I soon found that my body, which had not been nimble
in youth, resisted flexing with advancing age. I tried to
believe that the brain could send directional signals to the
chassis that would be obeyed. Not so. The feet don't move,
the eyes don't focus on the ball, the arms don't reach far
enough. To paraphrase a sage who must have tried to take
up athletics in the Third Third: "The mind is willing, but
the body is weak."

So we sports call each weekend morning to rally for the
workout. I, on the advice of elders, take a couple of aspirin
substitutes to fend off any complaining joints. If it is not
raining, I wish it were. I try to find an excuse for not meeting
to play, but she's wise to me. "No pain, no gain," I'm told,
and submissively, I acquiesce.

We agreed many years ago that reasons for not playing
well can only be used once a month and only recycled
once a year: I missed the ball because I was distracted
by the bird chirping; We went to a party last night and I
overindulged; I have a stiff neck from sleeping in a draft;
My glasses slip down in the heat and I can't focus on
the ball."

All possible excuses are brought into play and summarily
rejected. We don't speak the words of truth: "The old gray
mare, she ain't what she used to be."

A long volley brings temporary ecstasy coupled with the
agony of muscle pain.

A point well-executed is cause for celebration. We stop
and discuss the play and one of us suggests a recess, but
the other dutifully says that we're here for the purpose of
physical movement, not chatting. So back to work or play,
depending on the attitude, we go. Sometimes, though, a

caterpillar is in my path, and we both understand that it is a living, breathing reason to delay.

She wins more than I do, much more. A psychologist, my friend convincingly reiterates that we're engaged in this activity, so frustrating to me, only because we're extending our energies. Remember, "Use it or lose it," she admonishes. I never had it, I recall.

"It doesn't matter whether you win or lose, it's the game that counts," she says.

I respond with, "Show me a good loser and I'll show you a fool," but, in the depths of self-pity, I move on.

I'm beat by the heat. I'm defeated by my own ineptitude. I take lessons from a pro who patronizingly accepts my payment, but subtly explains that at my advanced age, she can't be expected to perform miracles, and there's little hope for improvement. Had I only started earlier, there could have been a better prognosis for progress. And I sadly acknowledge, "Too young, too old; too late, too smart."

My left knee aches. In the Third Third that knee cries out, "I've served you well for 65 years. Let me rest." But I'm heartened by the right knee, which has been there for as long, and is still behaving.

Because there is no one to listen sympathetically, I go on suffering in silence. It had better work. I'm investing in being an agile 90-year-old.

Only time will tell if the effort pays off.

Healthy Life Mends
A Tattered Heart

♦

Congratulations, Fred.

At 69, after a long, hard career in a construction-allied business, Fred retired this year to an adults-only condominum and is living it up. A survivor of a five-coronary by-pass, he is thankful to be alive, to be mobile, and to be able to live the good life.

He is enjoying this era of his life and the opportunity to attend to his physical well-being. Always jolly, in his Third Third he is more enthusiastic and bubbling than I've seen him in the 25 years we've been friends.

He starts each day by riding his bicycle for six miles or walking four miles. The pedometer strapped to his ankle responds to his body motion at each step and records the exact distance he covers.

His three cohorts await him at the tennis court upon his return, and they play a vigorous but friendly game for two hours. Fred is now seeded in first place for the tournament.

There are directed water exercises in the pool until noon in which he may participate, unless he chooses to swim.

After lunch is the well-deserved rest time at which he either reads or watches a baseball game on TV. Or visits with friends, or goes shopping.

The routine is broken only by a seafaring expedition on the boat he has docked at a nearby marina.

For breakfast Faye fixes Fred a citrus fruit, a half cup of fiber cereal with a half cup of skimmed milk. This is topped off by a slice of toast, lightly buttered, with one cup of decaffeinated coffee.

They collaborate about his diet carefully. She serves, and he eats, that which the American Heart Association recommends: no fat, plenty fruits and vegetables, pasta, no eggs, limited amounts of chicken and fish.

Although the AHA's diet guidelines don't prohibit meat, "Red is dead," says Fred. For protein he eats only that which grows from the ground, swims or flies. That which stands on the ground is a 'no-no'.

"Don't be a member of the Clean Plate Club," Fred says. "Forget about the poor children in India," he advises anyone who will listen. "It's us against them" he jokes.

They go out to eat twice a week and he throws caution to the wind. I've seen him indulge in both a highball and a scoop of ice-cream at the same meal.

He carries his ration of pills for the various internal, organic conditions his body is involved in. He takes his vitamins daily in measured doses.

As reward for his effort, when Fred goes for his regular check-up to his doctor, the response of his body is apparent. He has brought his cholesterol count down to 220 and is maintaining his blood pressure rate at 122/76. He retains the appropriate weight level at 174 pounds or Faye withholds the goodies, such as fat-free, but sugared and chocolate, cookies.

They have an active social life, which he can enjoy, now that there is not the pressure of work. He has joined a choir, rehearses regularly, and performs with them when they entertain the elderly in nursing homes. He dresses nattily and laughs a lot. He is the president of his 58 unit building association, but buffers any stress that might accrue to him with a complaint/suggestion box.

He is careful to go to sleep immediately after the eleven o'clock news (sometimes, he confesses, he drops off during) to assure a full night's rest.

Good for Fred. At this rate we'll have to take him out at 120 and shoot him.

An Insightful Event

♦

I n the Third Third the body begins to wear down a little here and a bit there. To keep going from now on, it's patch, patch, patch.

Only because I couldn't see out of my right eye did I submit to cataract surgery. This was traumatic, an act of faith, but well worth the effort. My underlying mistrust of the medical profession was, to a great extent, quelled.

The process that led to this drastic measure began with slowly deteriorating sight, so slow I didn't notice when the loss of vision became intregrated into my life. During regular visits to the ophthalmologist (more frequent to watch the condition of my chronic glaucoma) he hinted at the eventuality of removing the developing cataract film.

Once the announcement came that the cataract could be removed, the trepidation set in. The butterflies in my stomach really began to flutter about. Did I want to take a chance with invasive, intrusive measures when the doctor giving the second opinion said unequivocally not to do it?

There was not enough residual sight in the eye to justify

141

the surgery, he said. That meant I had a lot to lose, and little vision to gain.

A third doctor agreed the surgery was worth the chance. Then the two months of anticipation, nervousness and waiting began. Also, the prescreening exams, laboratory tests, medical-surgical clearance, the multiple visits, the multiple waits.

Finally, S-Day arrived. Armed with the cutesy four-color cartoon folder depicting 12 pre-op and seven post-op instructions, I'm ready to see what's ahead. I'm ready to submit to the wonders of modern medicine: the blend of human and technology. I enter the hospital for an out-patient operation on my eye. It's a simple procedure, I've heard. It just depends on who's eye is being gored.

I walked out three hours later: one hour of preparatory routines; one hour on the table; one hour of recuperation. I walked out groggy, thankful it was over, having committed my checkbook, insurance company and Medicare to more than $5,000. But how can we calculate the value of an eye?

The entire adventure was as pleasant as it could be for me, locally anesthetized and otherwise awake and aware that someone was approaching my eye with a knife. It was a well-performed drama, with all the actors doing their thing in the perfect harmony that comes from training, experience and self-confidence.

Despite the semi-comatose drugged perspective, I was impressed by the efficiency of the team, from the admission clerks to the surgical nurse. The use of robotics and the mechanization of the hospital made it seem like the latest space lab. This all added to the result of immediately releasing the patient with a minimum of after-effect.

Being the subject of this production was to be unspeakably awed by the advances in medicine and thankful that I'm living in a day when, at the age of 67, I can regain this invaluable possession.

The recuperation time was remarkably short. One week of lollygagging around and a few weeks of not bending or lifting were the only incapacities. The lens, implanted directly into the eye during the surgical procedure, saved me from "Dr. Cyclops bottle-bottom" glasses.

"We won," said Dr. Harold Stanley, my surgeon, my hero, as he shook my hand at the post-op visit. The 20/200 vision which I came in with now will be capable of correction to 20/40. What a victory for him, and surely for me.

"Will I now be able to draw in perspective?" I ask, using the age old line. He's ready with the answer, "As well as you ever could."

And I have my private concerns. Will my tennis game suffer because of the eye? Will I now see important things that for a lifetime have eluded me? Will I now see too much, more than I should?

I'm delighted with the outcome. I'm rarin' to go, unencumbered by the handicap of a sightless eye. I'm repaired and recycled with a warranty good for another 25 years of 50,000 miles. . .whichever comes first.

Whip Those Flabby Brains Into Shape

♦

Don't trash your mental capabilities just because you're in the Third Third. There's big hope for us to hold on to the smarts we had throughout, plus the promise of our ability to increase our mental capabilities.

Years ago the concept of retirement conjured up the notion that we would move from an active, productive life at age 65, to a sudden state of euphoria that was heretofore the substance of pipe dreams. We were programmed to be finished.

The implicit promise was that we would work for some 40 years, at a job too often detestable, stop work on the prescribed date, and suddenly enter the Magic Kingdom. There would be pristine clean, mechanical robots to perform our needed tasks, and we would not think for the rest of our life. B-o-r-i-n-g.

That theory was sold to us with the presumption that we in the Third Third would no longer want to, or be able to, think. Thankfully, new theories are coming from credible sources. They believe that not only can we maintain the level of cranial acumen we claimed in our youth, but, with a commitment to "working out" our brain cells, we can improve our mental stamina.

Memory loss and intellectual decline actually aren't part of normal aging until a person is in the 80s, according to Carl Carmichael, co-author of *Human Communication and Aging*. As people age they program themselves to aging prematurely, reinforcing sterotypes of old age, creating a self-fulfilling prophecy.

It really boils down to our choice of lifestyles. If we want to vegetate as we reach these years, we have the option to lean on the myth that supports the age-old idea that older people lose it, physically and mentally. Along come those who would debate that long-held misconception.

Recent findings suggest that mental well-being is like physical well-being: it can be improved through training. Mentally fit older individuals aren't "smarter" than other people, but they have learned to use qualities that each of us can develop. They have gained greater awareness and curiosity about the world around them, sharpened their problem-solving skills, and strengthened their ability to communicate.

According to Connie Lynch, a California psychologist, "If you start out simply, but with determination, you'll be amazed at the complex things you can do."

Dr. Lynch's workshops, for those over 50, accentuate improving mental functioning, memory and self-esteem, and protecting the mind from decline. She recognizes four key components of mental fitness: awareness, curiosity, ability to communicate and willingness to accept mental challenges. Approach new or controversial ideas with care and thought.

Paying attention to the details around you, changes and new ideas can increase your awareness. Use your senses: touch, hearing, smell, taste and sight. Use creative imagery.

Regain curiosity. Do puzzles of increasing difficulty. Read more on different subjects. Explore a new hobby. Flex those mental muscles.

"Those who remain active physically, intellectually and socially are most likely to not buy into the thought that aging is the doom of intellect and memory," Carmichael says. "So don't talk yourself into it."

To improve relationships and avoid misunderstandings, communicate and listen without passing judgment on what others say. Accept mental challenges: the brain will grow and become more efficient in an enriched environment at any age, according to Dr. Marian Diamond, a psychologist at the University of California, Berkeley.

Pay attention. A good memory is one of the fringe benefits of choosing a mentally active life. A realistic memory is to understand that you can't possibly keep track of everything.

We can't expect to generate greater mental capability than in youth, but if, as the experts say, we use it or lose it, let's go for the mental gymnastics. I'm not ready to give up thinking. I intend to keep on working out.

After all, the world needs some people who've been around and who know how to use the old bean. I'll not let it retire; rest it for a while, but not put it out to pasture.

Yesterday Visits Often

◆

Mayme Made Her Mark

◆

Recently I passed the supermarket that has a public bathroom which I call a memorial to Mayme, my mother. It reaffirms her belief and, consequently mine, that in America you can fight the system and win.

Somehow, in her citizenship training, Mayme learned that democracy is a participatory concept. She took on the personal challenge of shaping her little world with all her vigor, especially when her sense of justice was violated.

She was a little woman, more so as she shriveled into her 70s. But her activism, when she had a specific goal in mind, didn't wane until the day she died at 80.

In their Third Third my parents were physically and mentally very able. But a couple of times a year, when my family and job allowed, I would visit South Florida for a few days. It provided me a mini vacation, a chance to give each of them in-depth attention, and to catch up on their lifestyle and well-being.

Each morning Mayme would set out on her one mile "exercise" walk to do her marketing. She would buy one bagful of groceries so she could carry that home on the bus. The day I joined her in her ritual walk, as we approached the store at which she usually traded she said, "I'm boycotting them at this time." We went to another, two streets beyond, which she confessed to not liking as well. She reported the events that led to her drastic change of daily patterns.

It seems that, one morning, about four months before, as she was checking out her purchases, Mayme overheard another woman customer ask to use the lavatory. She was told there wasn't one for public use. That was the clarion call. "She was an old woman," said Mayme emphatically. "It was not right."

As Mayme decided the situation was unfair and unjust, she set about becoming the champion of that cause. Had I been nearby at the time, I could have warned the store manager to agree to a public restroom immediately.

As the story unfolded, Mayme announced to her card-playing girls (in those days grown women still referred to themselves in that diminutive way), "It's a crying shame the way they ignore the needs of old people around here. We've got to do something about it." The battle lines were drawn.

Every day, by plan, each of these women, all in their 70s or older, was to ask to use the bathroom. It was a simple enough assignment, so they all complied, and enlisted a cadre of other ladies from the apartment buildings in which they lived. Still, the manager was unmoved.

After a month Mayme, their leader, rallied the troops for a strategy change. They started a letter-writing campaign to their state legislator. Husbands (who in those days were thought to have more business letter-writing acumen) were drafted into the offensive. The state representative for their district referred them to their county commissioner who in turn sent them back to the state health department.

According to Mayme, "Little folks don't have as much

influence as a large food chain. But what's right is right."
So she was forced to call for a boycott. When the swing
of shopping modes became known to a competing store,
albeit one without public access to a washroom, but one
that enticed customers with attractive specials, the ranks
of the protesters swelled.

I had to return to my somewhat duller world. But Mayme
called me a month later, during daytime phone rates, an
act that indicated the importance of the message. "There
is now a clean, new, yellow and brown, tiled bathroom near
the entrance of my regular store," she announced victor-
iously. "The competitors are promising to follow suit."
Subsequently the code requiring a bathroom in public
places was more strictly obeyed.

When I passed Mayme's store last week, nine years after
her death, I missed her and, smiling to myself, silently
applauded her fortitude. I hope the people who use those
restrooms are thankful for the comfort.

Daughter's Birthday: Memories of Pain & Pleasure

◆

It's your birthday, my darling daughter, and I've done the usual gift, commercial greeting card and phone call to bring us closer together over the miles. But it's not enough as time grows shorter in my Third Third. In common with every mother, I wonder at the miracle I produced that is you, the woman of 43.

You started as a cherished gift from your father when, after following him at army camps, he was being shipped overseas to that frightening, long, hard war in Europe.

It was you and me against the world. I went to the hospital alone for your birth and called in visiting nurses to teach me how to bathe and feed you on a $52 monthly allotment for us both. At the only time in my life that I felt real poverty, I was enriched by you. You sustained me.

Even as I provided the creature comforts for you, you provided me with the capability of coping with the stress of your father being in five major battles. I settled into womanhood by caring for you and watching that cute, cuddly little doll develop into a person.

At war's end, that man came back into our lives, and you, aged two, had trouble making the connection between the photograph to which you'd been saying "Good night, Daddy" and the presence who threatened to put a wedge between us. Nor, to tell the truth, was he delighted with my preoccupation with my child, or with your kicking him in the shins, spilling on him, and telling him to go back where he had been. We put the pieces together in the jigsaw puzzle of our lives, fumbling every step of the way.

It could not have done your psyche much good when the baby brother, who arrived the next year, and whom you felt was another imposter, suddenly died. It was again a year of disruption in the smooth flow of family life.

My apologies for giving birth to another brother on the very day you left me for the first time—to go to school. It was a nasty trick of nature.

Later, you weathered the trauma of moving from one community to another, following the tempo of adult necessities you were too young to understand. You left old friends but learned the skills of adapting to new environments. You were caught, as we all are, in the conflict that flows from an individual's confrontation with the givens of our existance. You coped because you had to.

We went through, as everyone does, the times of "all my friends can stay up much later" and "they all get a bigger allowance." You were bothered by our seeming unconcern.

I hope we provided the security and encouragement for you to have an autonomous growth experience. But who of us, after all, is completely grown up?

Somehow you came through the angers of not having the clothes your peers found so important, because the family budget couldn't stretch. You did without TV because your parents felt it was an evil that would be a passing fad. It smarted, not having things amid a world of affluence. But you learned to work, earn your own way, and taste the pleasures of independence that would be an inheritance to last you all your life.

You couldn't believe that you had pulled *the worst, the very worst*, parents in the entire world who wouldn't let you, at 15, go with Roger (wearing a new uniform from a new war) to a drive-in to see *Peyton Place*. Those were the protective, tough-loving safety devices we imposed on you. At the time you considered leaving home, but we were thankful that something was at home to hold you.

Surely you must have some negative memories, as we all do, of growing up. We cast them off layer by layer as we mature and start to take on responsibility for who we are. You've come through with a value system of which I'm proud.

You managed to achieve what mothers wish for daughters: the joy of existence, the wisdom to know what you want from life, and the strength to get it. Each birthday brought the recurrent question, "How are you flowering into such an attractive and lovable person, in spite of us?"

We all played it by ear with that intangible, indefinable ingredient that evolved into the work of art that you ultimately became. Suddenly you were in college, graduating, with a prospective groom, and off to start life on your own. I was delighted we had made it, too.

Here you are today, too much separated from me, married 21 years and with two grown daughters of your own. My birthday wish is that they give you as much gratification as you have given me.

Just For The Record

♦

Eight of us, all women in our Third Third, were having our monthly tea-and-talk get-together and the subject of our discussion was love. Our hostess, Hildegarde, brought out her father's journal in which he had written about the joy he felt on the day she was born, and the family and world situation at that time. It was spellbinding and we could only speculate how much it will mean for that family's future generations.

What a great idea for today, for each of us to leave a legacy for our grandchildren long after we're gone. A brief record, on tape or written, would become the most treasured inheritance we could offer our progeny.

I'm starting to detail for posterity my life in the first and second thirds, eras that are unknown to them. I'll begin sorting the family history that I heard from my mother and father, and also my husband's family history.

I'll tell them about my Aunt Mary, a fashion designer who sailed to Paris twice a year and brought back such wondrous gifts as an umbrella with a hand-carved handle, and a pleated blue chiffon dress for me to wear for my first piano recital—a dress I ruined when I got sick from having to perform in Steinway Hall without talent. I'll tell them where I went to grade school, actually two miles each way from where I lived, and how I had to carry the container for milk to fill on the way back home.

I'll leave an outline detailing where each of my parents was born (in Russia and Poland); the stories about how they felt privileged to come to America; the unheated dwellings they lived in, and the night schools they attended. They ate boiled potatoes so they could move to a better neighborhood so that I, the firstborn, could attend a better school. Can I depict the pride my father and mother and their sisters and brothers displayed when I showed signs of belonging to the New World scene?

For the record, I'll note trolley cars, subway rides, twice-a-year movies, and the family trips to the opera. I'll try to relate the joy of taking a turn at my friend Muriel's home phone. She was the first of my acquaintances to have a phone.

Will they understand, or pass off as unbelievable, that until graduation from high school, 'nice girls' didn't go out at night alone. Can they comprehend that, in our teens, the country, and thus our families, were recuperating from the First World War, the stock market crash of 1929 and the depression that followed?

How can we describe the family holiday get-togethers when the women worked for weeks to turn the scanty food into delectable dishes? And the men, tired from their 12-hour work days, borrowing saw horses on which to make long tables of doors, and bringing 50-pound ice blocks into the bathtub to cool the drinks?

And the wedding for my cousin Fredl that had fresh grapefruit halves and sliced corned beef and squirting seltzer bottles? Will people who have so much now ever know the thrill we felt then?

Can anyone in the future enjoy, as my friend Sylvia and I did, endless hours of cutting paper dolls from the *Ladies' Home Journal* or sneaking a look at a forbidden picture showing the fetus in a woman's womb? Can they imagine a time when a ride in an uncle's car was an event that was anticipated for two weeks? Or an era when a newspaper that cost three cents was shared by three families?

I'll chronicle where I was when Lindbergh landed in Paris, when Amelia Earhart was lost, when peace was declared after World War II, and when President Kennedy was shot. I'll describe the winter cold in the house when the furnace went out, and being sent to Ella's, a mile away, to iron the blouse that had been washed and starched the night before and put on the radiator to dry.

I'll describe the unmitigated elation when our children were born; where and how we were living at the time.

Do others in their Third Third have similar fading pictures in the mind they'd like to preserve? Someone in the next generation, or the next, or the next, will want to know about the olden days. If not, nostalgia is its own reward.

My People In Pictures

◆

The house had a strange look when we returned after 22 hours in transit from a three week absence overseas. I walked from room to room, my mind gradually recognizing the familiar objects and their placement, familiar but with a gap from having seen and experienced so many other scenes on the trip. Everything at home seemed to be in order, but distant, as if I was visiting in another hotel, another museum.

Then the large wall of our bedroom that holds the family pictures brought a knowing smile of comfort. Of all the exhibits we had seen, here was the important collection. The pictures in the aggregation are valuable, worth looking at. This is my art gallery.

These are my people. There, with a large grin, I focused in on a display and was riveted to the old faded photos.

The arrangement is divided into periods. Someday I may get up the ambition to hang descriptive signs, as in the museums we visited, for those who will be viewing at a later time, without me to guide them. The signs will read:

'Too Old To Throw Away,' for those such as the portrait of my mother at twelve, with her mother, before she left Europe; 'Childhood of Arnie and Claire,' for each of our bare-bottom-baby pictures and formal poses with our families; 'Pre-marriage,' for those of our early adult lives. The next group starts with 'Our Wedding' in 1941.

On and on, around the room will be labels denoting the history behind our today. The largest section is for our children as they grew. That is when our reality began. This is the period when we two, Arnie and I, began to bring into existence our future in the form we wanted. In a sense, like artists taking a blank canvas and painting the pictures with our own design. These images depict our taking charge of creating our own life.

There is the picture of a holiday meal at my grandmother's table, with my doting aunts, uncles and our Madelaine aged 3, the first of her generation. Here is Arnie's father proudly pushing Jeff in the baby parade. And here is Mady's pretty little face swelled out of proportion by the mumps. This one is of the circus in our back yard with neighborhood kids and dogs dressed for their parts. There is the snapshot of Jeff in his fifth grade school play. And there is Mady in her first formal. I wear my heart on my wall.

The graphic record of their development, is like stopping time along the stages of metamorphosis from a caterpillar to a butterfly. There, statically framed, are the illustrations of their rapid changeover from infant to adulthood. There, in tintype and colored prints are presented the joyful years when we became a family, evolved through the ups and downs that each life must, and came through to the next stage. We have paper memories.

Madelaine's marriage to Ron, in 1965, is a landmark which started a new section of the pictorial record. Then follow their children and those of Jeff and Janice's family. Beautiful, clear art work that shines without further illumination.

We caught a great shot of Arnie, fully dressed in his Big 60 tee shirt, falling into the pool, pushed by our four-year-old grandson. Jeff strumming his guitar surrounded by our singing offspring. Papa, my father at 95, reading to a great-grandchild, already asleep in his arms. Our oldest grand-child's graduation picture is a reminder that she went off to college this year, and we guess it won't be long before there will be a new generation requiring wall space.

Of course, I've made the selection of what goes up there, sifting through the memories I want to recall. And why not? We want to remember the bounce and vigor of youth to carry us through these reminiscent days.

Anytime I'm discouraged with a happening of today, I take heart in viewing this graphic record of what we've produced, and it all seems OK. This show is the documentation of the passage of time, the panorama from our youth to now. It's as impressive as any studio arrangement anywhere in the world.

It's good to dawdle in pleasant memories. In the Third Third it's home, it's where we live.

A Reunion With Youth

♦

New Utrecht High School reunion? After 50 years? Who would be there? Whom would I recognize? What would we have in common? What would we say to each other? In the Third Third, why go?

Why not?

With great trepidation and careful makeup, I headed for the event in North Miami. Thousands of graduates of the Brooklyn, N.Y., school have migrated to South Florida. Two hundred and thirty-six of them attended the reunion.

After 50 years, a reunion is where you go to meet people who used to be the same age as you. It's where you go to bathe in water under the bridge. I went to meet the girl I used to be.

Those were the days of never having enough money to go to the 15-cent movies unless I walked the 53 blocks to school (really) to save the nickel subway fare, or worked for 35 cents an afternoon at the local five-and-dime.

In the distant memory are skipped heartbeats as Harold approached me; my fantasizing that he would ask me to

161

study for the trigonometry exam, but instead accepting his agenda of trying out for track. In those days, girls stayed mute about their desires. We delayed our gratifications, whatever we believed that to be, for "the right man" at "the right time."

I was awkward and gawky in those days when curves were a virtue, and I stood a threatening foot taller than many boys in my class. Warm waves of memory lap back of parties when we innocent teenagers postponed urges that teenagers throughout history surely have been subject to. We spun the bottle, and when we outgrew the peck on the cheek, we started dancing the Lindy Hop in an active frenzy that expended our energies in a socially acceptable manner. We did a lot of comparing notes, reviewing and embellishing experiences.

There were organizations. There were services. There were sports and languages and glee clubs. There was orchestra and marching band and the debate team. It was joyful, busy and a time that sheltered us from the cruel world of those Depression years into which we graduated in 1938.

Our innocent years came to an end as we faced unspoken concerns about reality. Too soon, most of the boys were men fighting World War II, while the girls waited to start their womanly careers of cooking, cleaning and bearing children.

I walked into the reunion with trepidation that my fond memories were distorted. The first of my classmates to approach me was Ruthy Bregman, who recognized me—with yearbook in hand. Seeing the picture there of me, Claire Furman, then an ingenue, was a dive into a pool of memories. I did a back flip when she reminded me that I would get dressed up to sit by the radio and listen enthralled to the crooning of Dick Powell.

Our reunion host Ray Rupelli recalled that I was the only girl in the band, a precursor to my feminism of today; and that I made a circle, if not very wide, having trained as the senior co-editor of the yearbook.

We left high school with high expectations, taking our own responsibility, our own significance in our hands.

The reunion was to honor Barney Hyman, the coach who retained the New York City track record for our school for 21 years. The men gathered to relive their sprinting, shot-putting, and running glories. We women, taught in those days to be supportive, applauded the retelling of each victory, but remembered only who went with whom to the prom, what she wore and who got engaged first.

About 10 percent of those in the room raised their hands when asked who had gone to college in those days of tight finances; most of them on athletic scholarships. Only three of us went on to higher education after we finished raising our families.

None of the crowd I had been close to showed up here. I'm haunted by where they could be, how their lives turned out.

We asked each other about old friends whose names we had trouble remembering. Some achieved great heights. Some died too young.

I didn't meet many I knew from 1938. But it was worth the day to reacquaint myself with that 17-year-old girl. I came away feeling she was not too shabby, but feeling, too, that you can't recapture youth.

That was then and this is now.

Colorful Characters
In Family Picture

♦

There was a festive spirit when we were in California for an early Thanksgiving turkey. "We get together so seldom," my niece said. "Let's take a family portrait." Thereupon, we got out the old photo album to review family get-togethers past.

One large, formally posed, professionally photographed picture showed the family in all its 1930s splendor.

"They look so stodgy and drab in a black and white photo when we're so accustomed to the brightness of full color these days," my niece said. I used to think so too, when I was her age, when I was considered "too young to know."

I recalled the rite of passage when my mother and her sisters considered me securely married, safe to be trusted with family stories. Not at all colorless were the people in the photo, embellished by tales and hearsay.

In the back row, his chin held rigid by the high, stiffly starched collar, is Uncle William, his hand on the shoulder of his daughter. He, a bootlegger during Prohibition, was a rich widower whose daughter eloped with "a bum who used her, abused her, and left her for Daddy to care for, tsk tsk."

To the right is Herbert, the wheeler-dealer, whose purpose seemed to be to help his brother William rid himself of his ill-gotten gains. "What's the good of having all that money, if you can't spend it or lose it?" Herbert would say. Herbert's schemes "came like trolleys; as soon as one was gone, the next one was waiting," the women in the family would say.

Seated in front of Herbert is his wife, Aunt Annie, whose goal in life was to fatten the family and anyone else who would dare sit at her table. She spent little time out of the kitchen, only what it took to maintain the home and to garner the food for the creamy rich menus she concocted.

Bachelor Uncle Maurice and his bachelorette sister Celia are next. She must have protested the seating arrangement for she disapproved of him and his lover, a married woman 20 years his senior.

Uncle Charles, hunchbacked, looks incongruous in a three-piece business suit, out of his usual costume of ear-muffed hat, scarf and lumber jacket which he wore to tend his newspaper stand at a busy intersection.

His meek wife, Min, sits with hands folded and with her thick glasses, "from reading every word before her husband sold it."

Uncle Nathan looks stalwart, the only man smiling, with an inner peace no one could understand. His wife, May, sits smiling too, but everyone knew why. She cooked, cleaned for, and was companion to two men in her home: her husband and her boarder, the photographer.

At the far right are Joe and Bertha who were not on speaking terms with the brothers at the other side of the photograph. All attended every family event, and sent messages to each other through neutral parties.

I knew these relatives intimately and remembered them,

and their anecdotes, well. I refrained from telling all. My nieces and nephews are too young to know the intimate details of the past; the skeletons in the family closets.

Besides, I want my niece to be kind as she tells future generations about the characters in this new portrait.

Wisdom Sustains

Mother's Myths,
Father's Fables

♦

My father died last month at 98. Although surely not a premature happening, nor a surprise, it created a change in lifestyle of no longer taking care of him and not having his supportive presence urging the Biblical injunction, "Choose life. Enjoy now."

Arranging his estate was simple. We paid the few remaining bills as we had been doing since he (a very wise man) exhausted all his resources four years ago. What our parents left—a cut-glass vase, a silver picture frame displaying their pride, and many books—were easy to divide with my brother. But haunting my awareness is the legacy of mother's myths and father's fables.

Last year, when I had a rare chance for a trip to China, I asked Papa if he thought it wise to go at my age, well over 60. "Of course, go if you want to see China," was his quick answer. "You'll never regret what you do. We only cry for opportunity wasted. Life is an orange."

Leaving him and riding down Sunrise Boulevard, I was stopped behind a bumper sticker that declared, "Life is a

beach." That was a new one that sent my memory traveling back to "Life is just a bowl of cherries," and "Life is a
Cabaret," and then, to my inheritance, Papa's story about
the orange.

When I was growing up and had a decision to make,
Papa, a mild mannered man, would wait for me to un-
burden whatever concern I would share with him, and then
answer with a lengthy parable. In younger, less patient days,
I would disrespectfully urge him to the punch line of his
tale. But as I matured and he, in my eyes, became wiser—
as parents do—I listened more attentively and incorporated
his message. Sorting through my legacy, I recalled the story.

Papa in his youth, an immigrant looking for a livelihood,
tried an apprenticeship with an itinerant salesman, Sam.
It was a career he abandoned after this first foray. They
brought the world to the isolated farmhouses of the newly
settling north Midwest. Sam would bring the pleasure of
his company, the display of the many sundry goods in the
back of the Model T, and a token gift for the family. This
time it was an orange.

The spellbinding part of the oft-told tale, as Papa
described that North Dakota family's reaction, was Sam
unwrapping the lustrous ball from the pink tissue paper
in which it had come from Florida. First the farmer un-
believingly said, "I have no need for that. That gold looks
costly. What is it?" Stealthily Mrs. Farmer came to look at
this object d'art glowing in the otherwise bleak kitchen.

"Don't be afraid. It's a fruit. For eating," Sam explained
as he offered each a whiff of the tangy sweet smell. Out
came the wares for sale: pots, checker board, pillows, all
of which were dwarfed in appeal by the dazzling orange.

One by one the children came to view this wonder of the
southern world, awed by the scope of nature beyond their
ken. Meanwhile, the order for Sam was growing. In an hour
the nearest neighbors' children were there to view the

orange. It was all right to look and admire, the farmer ordered, but no one, not friend or family, was to put a finger to it.

As Sam and Papa were ready to leave, Sam suggested the choice of juice or a slice, which could be savored by everyone.

"No, no," the farmer insisted. "You gave that to us as a gift and I don't want it hurt." Sam and Papa proffered the argument that the value and pleasure of the orange was in the consuming of it. "It's for now," Papa added. "Don't wait." Unbending, the farmer insisted that he would keep it in its natural state to show his brother's family.

The peddlers left—what else could they do?

On the return trek, six weeks later, they stopped at the very same farmhouse. "I'm so happy to see you," said the farmer's wife. "Something is wrong with IT." There on the sideboard was the orange withered, shrunken, with a trace of blue-gray mold coating the once shiny surface. "We should have tasted it."

As the traffic light changed, my decision was made. Papa, so long-lived, knew how fragile life is. I enjoyed the trip through China, remembering each day that "Life is an Orange."

Lessons
From The Laureate

♦

Mondays I subject myself to three hours in heavy traffic, but it's worth it. Mondays I'm like a lovesick schoolgirl. Mondays I attend a seminar at the University of Miami and sit at the feet of Nobel Laureate Isaac Bashevis Singer.

He's kind of frail-looking, this 81-year-old with the mischie vous smile to one side of his face. His elfin eyes twinkle as he tells about the goblins with whom he associates. He is a passionate man, and I enjoy being in the presence of passionate people.

He's unbelievably modest and shy, shrugging his shoulders saying, with a tinge of the Yiddish in which he thinks and writes, "I don't know why they choose me to lecture at a university English class. I don't even have a bachelor's degree."

More than 60 honorary degrees from schools all over the world qualify him for me.

I first met him when I returned from Kaifeng, China, where there is a small community of Jews. I brought him a translation of one of his books.

He is thrilled, like a child receiving a gift when it's not even his birthday. He invites me to lunch and I'm caught up with his magical charm. According to Dr. Lester Goran, whose lecturn he shares, "Isaac tends to pick up strays."

In hopes of gaining some pithy wisdom that will enhance my writing capabilities, I ask the obvious. "What makes you such a great writer?" With a shrug of the shoulder and a brush of the hand he states the obvious, "I'm not great. I just have a talent for writing."

As precious minutes slip by and I haven't yet gained the insight from the master, I ask, sophomorically, "How do you account for the popularity of your writing on such esoteric themes as the Jewish ghettos of Poland?"

He muses, as if this were his first consideration of that question. "People are curious about Jews," he answers. "We're an enigma." I'm quick to argue, "However, the Jewish population is dwindling into oblivion."

He responds with a powerful statement of faith, as we stroll along Isaac Singer Boulevard on a balmy day. The compelling effect of his courage impacts on me so that I want to stop and shout to the world, "Now hear this. I.B. Singer says, 'I have faith Judaism will survive. The lions are not so strong!'" And I try to believe him.

Maybe it is just this understanding and conviction that God, in whom he expresses deep faith, will ultimately tack a happy ending to the most tragic story of reality that gives Singer the unique perspective. Possibly, it is that third eye seeing hope, that is the essential attribute of a great writer. And the passion.

He arrives in the classroom in his running shoes with pant cuffs turned up, and starts to peel the banana he extricates from his secretive tote. He is ready to talk literature.

Professor Goran, who has been his translator and intimate for many years, begins to read from the manuscript of a short story Singer has just sold to the *New Yorker* magazine.

The writer strains to hear and demands, "Speak up. Slow down. Examine the words."

Goran cracks up. "I'll try. Is this OK?" he enunciates exaggeratedly.

Discussion about the story's meaning is elicited. We all participate in the heated dialogue while wondering how we dare venture our opinion in the presence of the work's creator. He gets the final word, as he must. "The writer does not make judgements," he states. "The writer's role is to describe the surprising complexities of the human condition."

With a sparkle that seems to be the genius shining out, he teases the young students. "When I was a boy, they called me a liar. Now they call me a writer."

After an hour a teacher is dry. Out of the bag comes a drink—cranberry juice in a box—the design of which he cannot cope with. We students vie for the opportunity to open it.

Once he finishes and publishes a story it is no longer his, he claims. The reader is welcome to interpretation. "It's only a story. If it's well written, entertaining, informative, precise, makes sense, and you read it to the end" he insists, "I'm satisfied."

Me too.

We've Seen It All, But We're Not 'Know-It-Alls'

♦

Unbelievably, it's a full year since *The Miami Herald* editor called to invite me to write a weekly column about the lives of people over 60. I accepted the assignment to "describe our activities as seen through my bifocals, with my own philosophical perspective." I chose to not seek the fountain of youth, but rather the joy in who we are and what we have in common.

"Tempus fidgets" when you're having fun and are keenly aware of aging. It has been a year of personal loss of people in my life who died because of age and, with each departure, I hear the bell toll for me. Is that what's causing the ringing in my ear?

But it also has been a very rewarding year of introspection and sharing my Third Third concept that these are the best years, if we allow ourselves to enjoy them.

The large response from readers has been gratifying as you take the time to call and write to agree or argue with my point of view. I'm particularly pleased about the feedback from those of you younger people interested in the subject by way of preparation for your future.

One message came this week from Esme Bauman, in which she writes, "Thirds. Why not fourths or sixths? Whichever, why is God so capricious as to grant us our fullest understanding and acceptance the closer we get to death? My answer to this conundrum would be contained in the ability of each of us to live for the moment. Now that I am well into my second third (or third fifth) of life, I find the age-old admonition of savoring the present, one of the most important and difficult philosophies to live by.

"This is not a hedonistic point of view, in my opinion. Enough people I should have reached out to are now gone from my life. As soon as this reality reached my gut, not just my brain, I consciously overcame my natural bent toward apathy and lip service and picked up pen and phone and took action. But not enough times nor toward enough people. I hope to grow.

"Youngsters are too busy surviving for me to expect my changing view of what's important to matter to them. There are two types of people left that I want and I need: my peers, my equals, my partners in this arduous quest to enjoy the moment; and my betters. . .

"I, the 'second third', am looking up to you, oh wise Third Third, but you better come through with some mind-expanding thoughts lest I dub you just older and not more venerable."

If I get your drift, Ms. Bauman, you missed mine. Your very words, "the arduous quest to enjoy the moment," are it. There ain't no more.

Don't look to me or any other Third Thirder for direction. We are just a few years ahead of you. We can only tell you what we've seen along the way. If there is a final conclusion, it is not pithy. It is simple and even simplistic: "enjoy today." Shakespeare, the Bible, and even that greatest of sages, 'anon', offer a variety of idioms, slogans and proverbs that add up to "today is the day to live."

We of the Third Third do not profess sapience. You who seek the answers to the eternal question, "what is the meaning of life?" will have to find it on your own just as we and generations of men and women have had to do.

We do not have insight or depth of knowledge by virtue of having lived more years. No automatic sagacity or acute discernment capabilities come as birthday gifts. At the stroke of 60 we do not each, suddenly, become a magus.

Nor do we expect your veneration by dint of our having been careful crossing streets for so many years. We don't seek respect on the basis of our endurance, nor deference for our mere longevity. We are not ennobled by the graying of hair or wrinkling of skin.

We want, though, your acceptance of our qualities and accomplishments. The law of probability favors our having made a place in the sun because we've had a longer chance to do so. Those of us who were wise in youth may, by now, have tempered wisdom with knowledge and experience, becoming people worth reckoning with. Others of us who were young fools are probably old fools, for we weren't smart enough to know the difference.

Comfort's Cost
Is Loss Of Freedom

◆

When Gloria called at the last minute Wednesday to say she couldn't join us for the annual foursome of lunch and theater, which had been planned weeks in adance, we were disappointed but not shocked. We've known each other since high school and have come to accept each other's ways. Gloria's foible is, "Joe doesn't want me to," and Joe's want is Gloria's command.

Gloria was a pretty girl whose mother told her, classically, "It's just as easy to marry a rich man." Gloria methodically chased, and allowed herself to be caught by Joe, the grandson of a "hardware typhoon." Her pursuit of happiness was ended early when she married Joe fresh out of high school. Lucky Gloria, she seemed then.

Throughout the 48 years since then, particularly in the early years of our marriages, the rest of us have had to struggle financially. But, here we are in our Third Third, having raised families and weathered the winds and hurricanes of our respective lives. Each of us has developed our own personality, choosing the person we wanted to be.

Gloria, the pretty girl, is now a handsome woman. Her good looks are enhanced by expensive clothes in the latest fashion, makeup fastidiously applied, and by an easy charm that takes her well into the social circles she frequents. At times when the rest of us were harried by the needs of our families, picking up kids at school, fixing dinner, preparing for home entertainment, Gloria was cool. She moved with a grace that spoke louder than she could tell—and she didn't—that there was someone at home doing those things for her.

Although she was modest about her wealth, her jewels, her country club activities, we envied Gloria. The feeling came when it would have been more comfortable to have hired help when we came home with a new baby; when the 7-year-old car I was so happy to get as a second family vehicle broke down; when the time came to commit for college costs. A family fund would have been welcome. But we had choices and lived accordingly.

Many times, though, we wondered about Gloria's decision-making, based on Joe's word, to which she was tied. She wore her hair long because Joe wanted it that way. She voted for candidates because Joe told her to. Her religious observance was Joe's way. She broke a date with us on Joe's whim.

Over lunch Wednesday, the word freedom came up. It brought to mind one of my papa's parables.

Once upon a time, a hungry wolf was wandering through the forest foraging for food, as wolves do. Suddenly he came upon a house and saw a dog. He walked over to the dog and said, "Hello, cousin, whatcha got in that bowl?"

The dog, seeing that indeed this was a relative of his, the same size and shape, just a little mangy and emaciated, replied, "This is delicious canine chow that the man in the house brings me twice a day with a bowl of water. Have some."

When the wolf voraciously polished off the meal, he looked at the dog again and asked, "How does your fur get so clean and shiny?" To which the dog responded, "They bathe me regularly and brush my coat."

"I'm so happy to make your acquaintance," said the wolf. "Let's enjoy an after-dinner romp through the woods. I'll show you *my* favorite spots."

"I can't do that," said the dog, and as he moved away to his doghouse, the wolf could see the collar and chain. The wolf ran off happily, untethered.

So do we three friends of Gloria wonder about being kept, and if the price is worth it.

Proud Parents
Pave Path

♦

We recently had a long long distance phone conversation with our son Jeff, who, at 38, has a major career decision to make.

"I'm thinking it through carefully," he told us. "I want to make sure I'm conducting myself like a man."

A *man*. Memories of Jeff's boyhood returned in a flood as we chatted across the miles. Jeff, reaching for his own value system. Me, so full of pride.

The first sign I had that my son was growing into manhood was when, as a high school freshman, he stormed into the house and declared firmly, "I'm not going back to football practice. I don't want to have my face stepped on, nor do I want to step on anyone else's."

His father and I had felt that Jeff, of burly build, was not athletic enough, so we urged him to put aside his records, reading of classical literature, and become a gregarious "big man on campus."

"No," the boy defiantly declared after the distasteful first experience, "That's not the kind of man I want to be."

He had been a sensitive child. In a dispute with his sister, he would yield to her, against his wishes, but maintain his rights and state that it didn't matter that much to him, and he'd rather please her.

The girls began inviting him to parties when his physique started to take shape, but he wasn't interested in them. Why spend time dancing when you could be playing the piano, he reasoned.

But one day, when he was 15, I came into the house and heard an odd sound upstairs. It was Jeff singing in the shower. "There's this girl in my math class. . ." he said and from then on, his life became a pursuit of women until he settled into marriage 10 years later.

His teens were full of youthful self doubts as he found his own answers, tasting, sampling, experimenting. The cost of the Woodstock experience was paid for with many hours of lifting Pepsi cases. The then new rock music, acid and sweet, threatened to crack the walls of our home, until he moved to an apartment on the University of Cincinnati campus. He defended the music as his language. We didn't understand the tongue, but recognized it as the developing vocabulary of his self-expression.

And there were other signs of his gradual maturation:

When protesting was fashionable, he called to tell that he was in New York City with his buddies, tight for cash, and having a wonderful time. They had been to a sit-in on Broadway that was great fun, just like in the news, with cops and water hoses, but he never did find out what issue was being challenged, and there were some great chicks and everything was OK and he'd be back to school next week and, "By the way, what does 'a la carte' mean?"

After one Thanksgiving dinner, when all the guests had left, Jeff asked to talk to us. In a somber tone, he told us that Jack, one of his friends who had been there that day, was no longer enrolled in school. He had flunked out two quarters ago, so he just stayed on campus, living in the same apartment, on the allowance his parents sent for tuition and room and board.

Jeff's question was about ethics. Would he be doing Jack more of a favor to "rat" on him or to shield him while he found his way. My boy was maturing well.

Recently, when I visited Jeff and his family, there was a heated discussion. His 13-year-old daughter wanted to be driven to tutor a home-bound child. Jeff was tired and chastised her for making commitments she couldn't keep. "But, Dad, it's for a good deed," she pleaded, "You always tell me to do good deeds."

"Sure," he answered, annoyed because he was weakening, "But you're involving me in performing your virtues." She seemed to understand his point, "but," she argued on, "I'm young and still learning." So he winked at me and, putting his arm around her said, "Let's go."

Now Jeff and his family have an important decision to make. He is an assistant high school principal and, rather than move up in administration, he longs to return to teaching, to write another musical with the kids, a sequel to the big hit they wrote last year. But choosing to not move up stifles his salary potential. As I listened to him on the phone, I remembered the glow on his face, the sparkle in his eyes, the tilt of his head, the guitar slung over his shoulder, as he rode away on his motorbike to his first teaching assignment with potential dropouts.

It's rewarding, in the Third Third, to see our children as grown-ups, facing grown-up decisions. Jeff has come a long way from the boy in search of moral principles.

I'm confident my son the man will choose the right direction.

Eleanor:
The Lady Was a Legend

◆

I n Lima, Ohio, I achieved my 15 minutes of fame, and am still remembered as the woman who brought Eleanor Roosevelt to town. "My Day" (the name of her column in the *Washington Post*) with Eleanor was Oct. 28, 1958, and now, in my Third Third, I'm left with anecdotes and memories that have had an effect on my life ever since. The First Lady of the World was my role model in fighting for women's rights and human rights.

"What must be done may be difficult, but can be done," Eleanor said.

Having covered a story about her years before in New Jersey, I was engaged to raise money for a non-profit organization by inviting her to speak. It was not a passive event.

The Right to Work Bill, viewed by some as anti-labor legislation, was an issue in many states, including Ohio, and Eleanor Roosevelt was on the air nationally in vehement opposition.

As advertising for her visit appeared close to election

day, passions flared on either side. A representative of industry in Allen County offered a $1,000 "donation" to cancel her appearance. We refused.

A large, influential advertiser threatened not to renew his contract with the TV station if I didn't guarantee to ask Eleanor Roosevelt to keep silent on the pending vote in her local media interviews. How could I deign to censor the words of such a person?

There was a threat on her life the day before she arrived. We asked for police help. The chief showed us the map and elaborate plans already in place for her visit. We felt both relieved at his foresight, and apprehensive that he had seen a danger we were too innocent to be wary of.

Her legendary warmth and indefatigable energy were evident as soon as we greeted her at the train (where Secret Service men were jumping off to hold the crowds away). She had agreed to stay at the home of a local doctor but asked to be shown around the community before going there. The drive through the tent slums of that rich area and the view of other notable sights interested her, and gave us a chance to speak woman to woman.

She asked about the schools, the cultural opportunities, what it was like to live in such a place. I, in turn, asked about her travels, her meetings with dignitaries, and her family.

Despite her renowned status, Eleanor Roosevelt was as warm and caring in private as she was in a large crowd.

When we finally got to the doctor's home, we found Tommy, the maid, asleep in a chair in the living room with a large soup tureen on her lap. She had been nervous about meeting this great woman, and about washing the very valuable antique piece, so the doctor had given her a tranquilizer. The guest of honor paid a great deal of attention to her all through dinner, and when Tommy cleared the table, she found a cash gift under the plate.

Rejecting the suggestion that she rest while waiting to leave for Memorial Hall, Eleanor Roosevelt said she preferred to get to know us better. We talked about responsibility in politics and how, in a democracy, we must all take an active role in support of our viewpoints. She placed a call to Carmine De Sapio, then head of the New York Democratic Party, and came back to the room saying she would have to leave for New York that night rather than stay over.

While she was on the phone, there were muffled voices outdoors. We, sitting in the living room, were concerned. It turned out to be the newspaper deliveryman being stopped by the policemen stationed outside. She chuckled.

The "performance" was a sell-out. Many who felt they wouldn't be interested in what she had to say later paid to listen to a tape recording in private. During the speech, a man rushed up on the stage and lunged for Mrs. Roosevelt. I was knocked over behind the curtain, and inadvertently buffered his thrust. Plainsclothesmen carried him away. She was concerned about me!

Undaunted, this giant of a person continued her speech after the interruption. She spoke only of her view of the future of U.S.-Soviet relations.

We chatted on the drive to the Dayton airport, and over the years I've held and cherished each word she said. From the well of memories rises the discussion about her children, who were then in the news because the public felt their behavior was inappropriate for the offspring of this illustrious couple. When I asked if she ever regretted that her family lived in a fishbowl, she seemed shocked by my naivete.

"One does what one has to do," she responded without hesitation.

"My dear young woman, you must learn," she advised me. "You pay a price for everything."

Old Age Just
A Stage of Life

♦

Arnie says I should hang up the tennis racket. He feels I'm getting too old to run around. "Relax," he advises. "Act your age." Now that we're solidly into our Third Third, he wants me planted on the couch next to him.

With the same reasoning, he tries to dissuade me from travels to China and Russia and wherever although, with a shrug of the shoulder, my mild-tempered husband of 47 years says, "Do your thing."

Ted and Thelma, contemporaries we've known for 40 years, came over to play bridge. Over coffee, the talk segued to vacations and became a heated dialogue between them. She won't leave the country with him because Ted had a heart attack seven years ago. "I have nightmares about being away some place and him pulling that one on me again."

Sure, sometimes she'd like to change her daily routine, but, Thelma says, "At our stage in life, it's too late."

Flory complains her husband Hal "is driving me up a tree" since retiring from the plumbing supply business he owned. A robust golfer of 70, Hal is on the greens four mornings a week when the weather is good, and he watches TV and is depressed the rest of the time. Flory finds an outlet in her volunteerism, but Hal ended work for pay, or not for pay, when he retired.

"Who would want me?" he asks.

Rose, a widow of 78, remains at home unless her children or grandchildren come to pick her up, wait for her to do her errand, then bring her back home. They openly resent the chore so she seldom asks.

There's no reason she couldn't do for herself except that she's afraid of being mugged.

Afraid of living for fear of dying.

Being scared of realistic possibilities seems realistic. Fear is a response we all have, appropriately, in the face of clear and present danger. But what is real?

Conversations with my father when he was 75—23 years before he died—inevitably led to his stating that he quit too early.

"I was so afraid I'd burn out, and now I'm drying out," he would say with a sadness about the chances he may have wasted.

"Live that you may live," said the Bible, which he was fond of quoting.

Lately, we've been hearing much about the newly-invented timepiece for young women, the "biological clock". Perhaps we have come up with one to define our age group, the "Stop the World, I Want to Get Off" watch: the ultimate stopwatch.

In 1933, Social Security was instituted for "older people", for the purpose of taking them out of the competition for the then-limited number of work slots. Now, with the extended life-span and the improvement in health, the 60s is too early for arbitrarily curtailing a career or other activities. Yet we have adopted age 65 almost as the law of the land for giving up active living.

The 65th birthday has become a signal for that stopwatch to sound the alarm. We begin to feel haggard. We're alerted to feel aches and pains. We listen for the hardening of our arteries. We forget an old friend's name and blame it on advanced age, although it also happened years before.

The 65 candles on the cake burn so brightly they can either light the way to new opportunities or blind us with the threat of suddenly succumbing to senility. Many quit risking and decide that challenges, fun and adventures are over. That stopwatch puts an end to going out or reaching out.

But not for me. I can reset the watch. There's too much to do before it's all over. I'll use caution to avoid being mugged. I'll be wary of safety because I don't see as clearly or walk as steadily.

There are those in their Third Third who have fostered a new absorbing interest in coin collecting, singing in a choir, taking courses in photography, music appreciation, sailing. I still have to take piano lessons and find a publisher.

The grim reaper won't find me rocking on the front porch, waiting to greet him.

Money Talks–
Can We Hear?

♦

One subject that comes up frequently in the Third Third is money. We're either worried or comfortable with the amount we have. We are concerned whether we will have enough to last out our years now that our earning capacity has waned. And we wonder what to do with the money we don't spend.

The consensus: Money talks, money is power, money is control and money can create a problem.

I was raised in a family where there was little, so money talk was considered crude and money was sarcastically referred to as "the almighty dollar." Among the virtues to be pursued were honesty, loyalty, courage and thrift, but never money.

As we know, we must plan for the inevitability of our deaths. Nobody really wants to face it, but we all subconsciously know it is in the not-too-distant future.

How far in the future is the persistent question.

At this age, we are less acquisitive, thus we can become more generous in giving away some of the uncommitted funds. But the fear of illness or incapacity or inflation restrains us from giving too much away.

Money symbolizes security. There is the thinking that we can extend our good life by accumulating dollars.

The person who has a bulk sum that was acquired by means fair or foul commands a certain amount of respect. Those who have amassed an abundant quantity are not necessarily smart, likable, or admirable—or are they? Those of us who are convinced we can't take it with us wonder about how and to whom to leave it. Mavens, to whom money matters matter, advise that we must make the statement, and etch it in writing now, while we're in control of our mental faculties. What shall we say?

We have the choice of leaving our entire estate, whether it's $200 or $2 million, to our spouse. If it's sizable, the Internal Revenue Service will take a big bite. Patriotic though we are, few would want to give Uncle Sam a gift, by will or default.

By leaving it to our children after the spouse is gone, we are telling them we love them.

Should we distribute among our children according to their needs or according to our feelings about them? When they inherit our assets, it can affect their lives.

We could leave some or all our money to charity or a cause in which we believe. That could speak louder than words about what we stand for.

We could leave a large sum to someone other than family to say, "Thanks for making my life more pleasant." We could make an award to an unfortunate person to whom fate handed a bad break.

Is the only proper thing to do, according to societal mores and legalities, to unquestioningly leave one third to our spouse and divide the rest among our progeny? What if an adopted child or one who came with a marriage is dearer?

When we leave our estate, huge or tiny, is it as a reward?

If money talks, I wish it would speak up so we know which way to dispose of our fortune. I wish it would speak up soon and clearly, for I'm already getting a little hard of hearing.

You Can't Buy Happiness, But Americans Sure Do Try

♦

It's that time of year when the shopping centers lure like a giant magnet drawing from a wide field of power. The variety of goods, necessary and otherwise, glamorously displayed, dazzles and explains why people all over the world learn of our plenitude and want some.

My friend and I find a parking place and stop for lunch. "I feel depressed," Edith says. "I want to send my children something for the holidays, but I can't imagine what they don't have and I can't afford what they can."

Her husband is a retired detective who, at peak, earned less than the $25,000 starting salary of a policeman today. She worked after the children went to high school, but didn't accumulate enough for Social Security on her own. Her son is an attorney whose first job out of law school with a prestigious law firm paid him $45,000.

Her daughter-in-law, a bank branch manager, works because the couple can't, or won't, make do on his income alone. Two children, 6 and 10, soon will become teenage consumers.

194 ◆ The *Third* Third

"You just don't understand," her son tries patiently to explain. "We need things."

They don't speak about enjoying their work. They seem to be caught up in prosaic pursuit of material articles. If anything, Edith bemoans, there's a single-mindedness about making money. The purpose is to accumulate big toys.

"I want to give them the gift of dreams, pride, purpose, dedication. I want them to care about other people. I want them to live by the Golden Rule. I feel bad about having raised a son who is so crass," she says.

We consider if it's the upbringing or the environment or the times. It's the question of nurture vs. nature. We determine that there is no definitive answer.

Edith's son is not unique. He lives in a community of similar people. When she visits, she's introduced to one after another: clones with clean fingernails and MBAs.

They can't keep up with their expenses, nor does that seem to be a goal. No sooner do they pay off one charge account, than they get visions of sugar plums dancing in their heads, and they buy, buy, buy. It's their America.

In their 30s and 40s, their party talk is about travel to "in" fashionable places of the world that we have never even heard of. They don't go to see the wonders of the world or how other people live. They go now, pay later, to be able to tell each other they have been. They go as relief from the stress of paying for their way of life.

The grandchildren say, "I need, I need, I need" when they mean, "I want, I want, I want."

As a mother, Edith is pleased that her family has the necessities plus what it takes to be part of the scene. She is a member of the League of Women Voters, Common Cause, and other groups concerned with betterment of society. She confesses to wishing her son would talk about, and thus impart to her grandchildren, values that would set them up as good citizens.

She closes the conversation as we trudge off to view the tinsel and lights and to buy gifts, bordering on the obligatory. "The last time I visited, my son was wearing a T-shirt that read, 'The Golden Rule: He Who Has The Gold Makes The Rules'."

Good Grief

♦

The phone call was the same as the visit had been four months before. Dorothy, the widow, was grieving. What is there to say? What is there to do for a dear friend who has spent the past six years mourning her dead husband?

I realize that I cannot judge the valley of despair without having been there. But because we are friends and she turns to me, I urge her to cooperate with time and to seek counseling.

In contrast, Ruth, more recently widowed after having been married for more than 40 years, is going on with her life.

"I loved him when he lived, but he's gone," she states with affirmation. "I have to go on living."

It may appear harsh and unfeeling to say, but the difference seems to be in the mourning process. Both women are bright, intelligent and outgoing. Both had good marriages to men they loved and respected. Both have families, friends, skills and other resources to tap.

According to Gale Bouchillon, a specialist in separation

and loss at Nova University, there are four stages of grieving that are common: shock, anger, despair and resolution.

For most people, the loss of a wallet or a theft will lead to feelings of loss. Obviously, they are shorter and less intense than the grief in losing a loved one.

Initial shock becomes disbelief, keeping a stiff upper lip and denial. People in this stage hide their feelings.

The anger stage brings blame. Many dredge up reasons to feel guilty. Feeling victimized, they ask the recurring question, "Why did this happen to me?"

Usually despair follows, and the widowed ones become depressed. They can't accept the loss. "I'll never smile again," is a frequent attitude at this stage.

Then there is the resolution that allows the grieving person to begin, in slow steps of growth and development, to regain self-confidence and a desire to go forward.

For those who progress through these general movements, there's a light at the end of the tunnel. For some, this can take six months, for others, perhaps two years or more.

Some, who had difficulty coping with life before, may remain fixed in one of the stages and find comfort in seeking understanding, even empathy, there.

Patricia Gershwin, a twice-widowed psychiatric social worker specializing in work with widowed persons for the Mental Health Association, suggests the process not be rushed. "Time is the ally," she points out, "if the grieving one wants to come out of it whole."

It helps to have an ultimate goal. It helps to be in the company of those who have successfully resolved their grief. It helps to find a redirection. It helps to connect with someone, a friend, a lonely elderly person, a child to give warmth and caring. Even if it involves a cat, a bird or a plant, it helps to be needed.

Some who have suffered a loss turn to, and get strength

from, their religion. Some become stronger and able to be more self-expressive. There can be a sense of release from treating an ill mate and relief from the confinement. For some, once the separation and loss has been dealt with, it can be a challenging era that brings freedom and satisfaction.

It can be the beginning of the rest of a good life, acknowledging that the lost one can be kept in the most favorable light. They can go on with pleasure and adventure while treasuring loving memories.

As for Dorothy, I don't really know what it's like for her because no one can ever experience another's grief. I can only wish her an accelerated trip through the passages of recovery.

After Today

♦

Now's The Time To Sit Back And Savor Life

♦

"**M**y sister watches the soaps almost every afternoon," said the woman sitting at the back during a talk I gave to a women's club recently. "How can I motivate her to get out into the real world?"

Before I could collect my thoughts, a similar comment came from another member of the audience, also a well-dressed, well-coiffed and well-spoken woman: "Where I live the fashion is to play cards. Is that any better?"

What were they saying? We had been talking about time. I had tried to make the point that at this age we have fulfilled the tasks we undertook as young brides: to love, honor and cherish our husbands, to raise children and care for them, to conduct a social life, and to generally run a smoothly operating institution, the family. In the Third Third our time belongs to us and, feeling comfortable that we have done our jobs well after our nests have emptied, we can pick up on those things we have always wanted to do.

Our youth, in the first half of 20th Century America, came at a time of transition. We were at a point in history between the enslavement of our grandmothers and the freedom of our daughters. Our grandmothers had uncontrollable numbers of children without resources to care for them, while our daughters are able to plan the size of their families and have careers.

When we reached adulthood we were already breaking the bonds of the house. Men, who really started the women's movement, made the machines that freed us from the time-consuming, heavy labor of home maintenance. The vacuum cleaner got us off the floor. The refrigerator allowed us to store food for longer periods, ending the daily shopping trips. The clothes washer and dryer gave us a day a week; non-iron fabrics gave us another.

We enjoyed each invitation to leisure as it was presented, but we sensed the truism that freedom is the most difficult concept for humans to cope with. We housewives had no patterns to follow, no role models. We didn't even know the choices that were available to us. It required an entire generation with the luxury of time on its hands for American women to believe that this most valuable commodity, time, was really our own, to spend at will.

We began to explore the world around us, leaving the house for short periods. We volunteered for charitable causes, with the justification that we were being virtuous in getting dressed up and going from the confines of where we were previously tethered. We would go downtown shopping allegedly to save large sums of the family budget. Meeting a friend with whom to share the experience was an added bonus. Middle-income women formed organizations for a variety of stated purposes; unstated was the desire to be with other women looking for an interesting occupation to fill the free hours.

Many found hobbies that grew from avocation to vocation, while many found the non-programmed time created a problem. As we and the century matured, new avenues opened for us. Occupations considered unusual for women in the 1940s became acceptable. Women who accomplished their goal of child-rearing moved into new and exciting directions.

Jeanne Faiks, mother of five, started law school at 56 and is now a practising attorney taking time out to travel. Ann White, while her family was growing, visualized an alternative theater in which to present innovative concepts, and is now receiving standing ovations for her productions.

Irma Rochlin believed the saying, "A woman's place is in the House and Senate" and became a Florida state legislator after her four daughters went off to their own lives.

Nor does this opportunity to take those dreams off the shelf where they were stored while we were cooking, cleaning and caring for measled children mean that we make such dramatic moves. To each her own. Each of us does at her own pace to fill her own time.

Now, finally, we have choices without obligations. We can take courses in art appreciation or play cards. We can learn to play golf or write the poetry that came to us 30 years ago in the middle of waxing a floor. We can read the classics that are faded at the back of the bookshelf or we can take tap dancing lessons.

We now have the freedom to do anything we choose as long as it doesn't impinge on someone else's freedom. There are no shoulds or coulds, no rights or wrongs, no judgments. Our time is our own and growing short. If we're ever going to live those fantasies, now is the time.

We must number our days while we can.

Aging Children Anguish
As Parents Linger

◆

"I want to run away from home," cried my friend who I will call Fran. I hurt to see her, a pained 61-year-old who burst into tears as we rode to the theater and told of her family situation. Her husband, thankfully on the way to recovery after a recent heart attack, her daughter's rocky marriage, and concern for grandchildren, niggled at her. And her 87-year-old mother, incontinent, in pain, in a nursing home again, asks daily, "Why don't you come visit me more often?"

"I'm so ashamed of myself," sobbed Fran. "What kind of person am I who can't love those who are nearest and dearest to me?"

It seems she just finished raising her children, getting ready to begin to live her own life, to travel, to take some courses, to attend theater, when she finds herself in this bind. It's a familiar Third Third story called "Tales of the Sandwich Generation."

It's familiar to me because my colleague Bettie, a widow, told me that, again, she couldn't leave for her planned vacation because her mother had just broken her hip. Her mother's mind has been crumbling away for a long time.

It's familiar to me because in the last three years, as my husband and I have struggled with the same soul-searching, we have put to rest three of our parents, aged 95, 95 and 98, for whose care we had been responsible.

The frail elderly are living on in the zone between life and death, kept on the brink of life by the artificial technological and chemical sustenance that few favor except the industry that has mushroomed and profited in recent years. The professionals in the field of elderly care take no responsibility for the psychological impact on the families; they just take the money. Much money.

"It breaks my heart to visit my mother and helplessly witness her deterioration, day by day, knowing there's no return, feeling it's time for her to go," Fran sobs as she self-consciously exposes her inner turmoil. I drive on, feeling her feelings, and wishing there were some promise of relief.

But I see only a morass of deeply sensitive and private relationships interfacing with cold government regulations and calculating deliverers of services. The moral dilemma raises pithy questions about 'who cares for those whose lives are already spent, and for how long, and to what extent?'

The guilt is enlarged by remembrances of our grandparents being cared for, whether dutifully or lovingly, in the home. Then families lived closer so Aunt Bertha would come over to share the load. Then, before today's man-made interference, few fragile parents lived into their nineties. Our lives, we reflect, were more in the hands of God. With fewer choices, there were fewer problems. Or so it seems.

Sisters and brothers discuss parents' welfare over hot long distance lines. The out-of-town sibling seems to have sage advice about the proper care; the on-sight caregiver, usually a woman already in the Third Third of her own life is resentful. She feels she is being used by the rest of the family, ensnared in the system, and sandwiched into the trap of time. There's martyrdom coupled with concommitant guilt. "The others show such concern. What's the matter with me?"

As we drive to our destination, Fran and I discuss the elements of the problem. We are aware it is a sign of our time, our generation, and our culture, without answers. We know it will become worse as science and morality continue to clash.

By the time the parents finish these long goodbyes, the children's feelings are so confused that all the emotions, efforts and caring, are buried under a heap of exhaustion. Surviving only is the burden of guilt at not, ultimately, having done right and fulfilled the Biblical command to honor thy father and thy mother. It's a "no-win" situation unless we know in our heart of hearts that we did what we had to do.

The conversation has helped Fran purge her guilt in a river of tears, for a while. She takes her make-up from her purse and begins to repair the damage to her face, preparing to go forward and deal with her life as it comes.

In closing the discussion she asks, "Who will care for us?"

The Hurting Spot

◆

Recently, after I suffered a traumatic loss, I had one of those stressful days that everyone has once in a while. Those times have a way of seeping into life more and more as we move into the Third Third.

More of those whom we love go the way of all flesh. We witness more world and personal tragedy, finding ourselves with fewer resources as we age, fighting harder to stay buoyant. We must be philosophical about it.

I take my philosophy of life from fortune cookies and bumper stickers: "When the going gets tough, the tough go shopping." So I went to the grocery store to find some herbal tea.

As I turned down the paper goods aisle I met my friend's sister, whom I'll call Janet. It's a good thing I hadn't yet bought frozen foods, for they would have melted during my talk with her.

"Not well," she said when I asked how she is. She made the point that nobody understood what it was like for her to lose her husband two years after he retired.

"We waited all of our 43 years of marriage to finally start to enjoy life," she said with a tremor in her voice that promised tears would quickly follow. "What's left for me?"

Unfortunately, it's a cry common from our age group. I tried to be sympathetic to her plight, but found it difficult. It had been four years since Janet became a widow.

Further saddened by the encounter, I drifted mechanically up and down the aisles, pleased that for me this funk feeling is rare. Although my loss was not to be compared in magnitude to hers, I've had my share of grief, as has each of us who has lived to reach the Third Third.

Once again I was reminded of the old saw about the patient who comes to the doctor for advice: Every time he puts his right hand to his left ear it hurts. After a thorough examination the medic advised the patient, "If it hurts when you put your right hand to your left ear, don't do that."

No one else can help Janet, mostly because no one else knows where it hurts her, or what will make her well. It isn't that the people who love her don't care, they don't know what to do for her. Because they love her, they want to believe that the agony is easing up, that her wounds are healing. Also, what Janet doesn't seem to acknowledge in the litany of her suffering is that everyone, including her children, her sister, her friends, is busy with their own life. And their own pain.

She seemed so self-involved as to negate any problem but her own. In the kindest words as I could, I suggested that if it is so uncomfortable where she is, she get off that spot. She could call a senior service to talk to an uninvolved listener. Or better still, she could go there and become a listener.

When I get to feeling stress from a major trouble, I go to the beach. My concerns are dwarfed in minutes by the ebb and flow of the ocean, which has been there and will go on despite my aches and others' problems. Minor woes are helped by an ice cream soda.

My friends report a variety of methods for "Moving off the hurtful spot." I wouldn't go as far as one who gets out her Jane Fonda exercise tape and bends till she drops. But I do turn on an old Artie Shaw record and jitterbug to the beat of "Begin the Beguine".

My neighbor knocked on my door the other day with a bowl of lasagna. "I was feeling so depressed this morning, I wanted to feel successful," she said with a smile. "So I got out my good old recipe and made some for each of the neighbors." I was glad to be the beneficiary of her attempt to change her mood.

While she doesn't need the money, another friend has found working a part-time job helps her cope with the loss of her husband and child in an auto accident. Another, who lost a son in Vietnam, volunteers as a tutor in the local high school.

The days of Janet being needed by her family are gone. We can't bring back the good years when your lives were whole and in control. But there can be good years ahead in other times, other forms, other places. We can find a new role in which to be needed. The choice is ours to stand where it's uncomfortable or move away. We can, for the moment, for the day, or forever, try to get off the hurting spot.

Today Is
The Rainy Day

◆

I t was a ridiculous argument, as are most that "other" couples have. This couple is modest, quiet, middle class, married a long time, in their 70s, part of our social set.

As they got into our car they seemed to be continuing a battle that would go on and on. It appeared they were arguing about how long they would live.

"As usual," she broke the ice, "he doesn't want to go out to dinner."

"And she'd go out to eat every meal," he fired back.

During dinner, the skirmishing erupted again. She claimed that since he had retired, he had become "tight." He had been responsible for family financial matters, and now must see to it that they had enough for their old age.

Although he was the breadwinner when she was a home-maker raising the children, his job ended the day he took the gold watch. He has hobbies, helps with some minor household duties (which are basically hers), carries the groceries in from the car. His role is to give himself pleasure.

"Man works to dusk from dawn. Woman's role is never done," she said. That was a proverb my grandmother, hardly a feminist, taught me.

"I don't need to eat heavily every night," he explained. "I just want her to make a simple meal."

"The simplest food is to simply order from a menu," came the ready retort.

She wants to make her life easier as they age, too. As their energy wanes (and we must be realistic that energy wanes as we age), she wants to purchase help. Just as they used to buy goods, they now need to buy services.

With one car to share, he refuses to take, or allow her to take, an occasional taxi when their separate schedules conflict. She finds the bending that housecleaning requires too difficult and wants to hire a younger person twice a month to make that effort. He feels they can do it together.

"Ha, how many times has a man cleaned a toilet?" she said. From his grin of admission, she has hit the mark.

When the temperature drops two degrees, he turns off the air-conditioner, although he too feels the discomfort of the heat. Travel and theater, other ways in which she wants to spend her retirement, are to him frivolous, unneeded expenditures. She said the economies are always made at her expense.

Both worked to build a nest-egg against the uncertainty that they would face at this age. His position is now that earnings have stopped, they must conserve resources. "The money tree has dried up. It no longer bears fruit each year."

When the children were educated and off on their own, they were able to save money. With Social Security and a modest pension, they are able to live without using their savings.

"He is still saving for a rainy day," she defends her point. "I want to use it for the sunny days while we still can."

Most of us have established a new comfortable way of life for our Third Third. We've reduced our housing, our entertainment, our purchases. We have adjusted our mode of living to our income, large or little, and find comfort with peers in similar financial situations. It's a good life.

"Sure," he says. "That's fine as long as you're healthy." We know he's on target. Today, with the "threat" of increased longevity, neither we nor society have a trustworthy plan for coping with the last of life. Each of us has a recurring nightmare that longevity will leave us helpless with terminal illness.

Most of us have Medicare to pick up much of the constantly rising cost of medical care. But each of us, with few exceptions, is concerned about the long-term illness that can wipe out a family's finances completely.

Comparing notes, we found that we both carry the catastrophic health insurance that is designed to ease the burden of major sickness. The rest we must leave to our government and fate. We must pray, and help by proper diet and exercise, to live vigorously and die suddenly when our time comes.

But knowing we can't take money with us, the trick is not to leave too much behind.

When Kids Grow Up,
The Silence Is Deafening

◆

I t appeared in the media that Mama Maria Gorbachev complains about her boy Mikhail. She never sees him. "He never visits. He never calls. He never writes," she's quoted as saying.

That lament is familiar in the Third Third, especially when sonny boy is in a distant city doing things like making a living for his family or running a government. First let's establish that "never" in Mother Tongue does not mean at no time: It usually means not enough.

What mother, miles away from her kids, can't relate to this?

The joke making the rounds these days goes like this: Four women sit down to play cards. One says, "Dear me." The second sighs, "Oh, my gosh." The third whimpers, "My aching back." The hostess reminds them. "Today we weren't going to talk about our children."

Ha-ha.

Blame it on Henry Ford. Or Robert Fulton. Or the Wright brothers. They are the ones responsible for stepping up transportation systems. Our kids, like everyone else in this mobile society, just took off for distant places.

But did they lose their way? Doesn't the car, the boat or the plane go home the same route it left? Apparently not. Once the chicks leave the nest, they're off on their own into a new, absorbing world that we are not a part of.

Explaining why she is remaining in the same small village, rather than moving to Moscow, the "First mother of Russia" explains: "I don't see my son here, and I wouldn't see him there."

Mrs. Gorbachev, widowed, is said to occupy her time with chores around the house, baking bread and watching her new color television set, a gift from Mickey.

When parents adapt to the relaxed level of life after raising their kids, that doesn't necessarily fill the need to hear from them.

We, the current Third Third generation, have been through so many changes we didn't have a chance to catch our breath. The more communications became advanced, the less we were communicated with.

When we were young, the phone was at the candy store down the street or at the home of our rich aunt. Phones are now in every room including the bathroom, in cars, at tables in restaurants. We have the means of reaching out, but the important calls are often slow in coming.

Mail that in our youth took three weeks to get cross-country now automatically goes via air mail. Overnight express mail, fax and computer modem messages get the buzz to us as soon as the sender thinks it.

Telecommunications is the event of our time. Satellites bring us pictures and messages from around the world. The opportunity to communicate is as open as *glasnost*.

But have we really missed the big picture? The more we say, the less is said. We have mountains of words coming at us daily in newspapers, magazines, junk mail, phone lines, radio, billboards, TV and sky-writing. We're inured to the massive number of words beating at us, and we're becoming tuned out.

We've helped our children to become educated. They have degrees in fields we never dreamed of. But even the B.A., M.A., M.B.A. or Ph.D. degree never taught a course in correspondence with parents.

Maybe the medium is not the message between the generations. Maybe these are not the means for mother-child relationships to connect. Maybe mothers can get the message that the children care about them without saying a word. Maybe the less they say, the more they feel a closeness and a tie. Maybe the silver cord is really a telegraph cable that doesn't need a formal code.

No matter how improved the lines of communications become, we moms never get letters from kids. Well, hardly ever. Surely not ever enough.

We're Off Our Rockers

Call Me Old And Fading, But Don't Call Me Out

◆

I'm old.

This week I celebrated my 66th birthday, and there's no getting around it: 66 is certifiably old.

There's something good about knowing who I am, and knowing I'm old, that puts a perspective to life that has merit.

Last year, when I turned 65, I wasn't ready to make this statement. I had to wait to taste it, to live it, to experience being so far into the Third Third that there's no turning back, no denying, no forgetting. You have to let the words roll around your tongue for a while to feel like it really belongs there—to be able to say, "I'm old."

It kind of creeps up on you.

Not only do bag boys automatically assume I need help, but they call me "Ma'am," a term that seems to be reserved for the doddering.

Ma'am is one of the acceptable appellations. It's OK, along with euphemisms such as elderly, mature, in the advanced stage and along in years.

I'm full-grown, past my prime, no spring chicken.

I'm silver-haired, wrinkled, fading. I move a little slower and my eyes are going. But I'm not ancient, hoary, decrepit, infirm, tottering, fossilized or on my last legs.

I'm senior to many people who were born after me, but I'm not necessarily venerable. Just because I've been careful crossing streets, taken my vitamins regularly and outlived many of my peers is no reason for you to hold me in high regard. Respect me, if you will, for who I am and for having made the most of my opportunities.

I'm getting on, in my golden years, even seen better days, but that's not all I am. I am a woman who carries with her 66 years of accomplishment, of successfully coping with life's exigencies. I've given birth to and reared children, given them a set of values to carry them into an independent, comfortable way of life. I've been a lover, a wife, a nurturer. I've been devoted child to my parents and friend to my friends. I've had a gratifying career, volunteered in the community and made contributions to society.

I have the wisdom that comes with having been around with my eyes open. I know how to laugh heartily when something is funny because I've encountered sadness. I know that to stay out of debt, no matter how tough things are, is to maintain dignity. I know that it's easier to obey the law. And I know a few more things.

I'm the one who knows enough about war that we must never have another. Whatever it takes. Never.

I will not apologize for my age. Everyone has to be some age. It's ridiculous to engage in the futile effort of wishing we were younger than we are. Our only hope is to be older.

When we were tots or teens there were problems and pleasures. When we were youths striking out to meet the world on our own, there were pros and cons. When we were newlyweds and beginning to do our thing, we rushed the minutes away. Slowly, slowly, things fell into place.

The kids had to move out on their own, and soon a spouse will be gone. But that's life, that's what happens while you're making plans.

It doesn't really matter what the bag boy thinks of my stage in life. At his age, what does he know?

It matters more that, at my age, I know about what great joys can be his if he learns to live each day to the fullest. And it matters more that I have enjoyed, and have memories to look back on, and prospects of all sorts of pleasures ahead of me. There's still time to be bold.

I face the fact that I'm old. But don't count me out, yet.

I look forward to this, the Third Third, however long it may last. We triumph who savor the sweetness.

This is, indeed, the best time. I can rest on my laurels, free of anxiety, and let the bag boy carry out the packages and place them in the car for me.

I might as well take full advantage of being old. If you're called the name, might as well play the game.

Dare To Dream

♦

On a Tuesday afternoon in April 1974, I stood at the top of the broad marble staircase in the administration building of Florida Atlantic University with tears streaming down my face.

Dr. Robert Tata, the department chairman, had told me a few moments earlier that my thesis in urban geography had been accepted and that I virtually had a Master's degree.

I was 54, four years after starting from scratch at junior college. What would I strive for next after my lifelong dream of education had been fulfilled?

Dr. Tata patted me on the shoulder and reassured me that I would find another goal, and he said to go for it. Well into the Third Third, his words ring true. Dreams keep coming and fulfillment follows, regardless of age. Surprisingly, the rewards are here. We need only the audacity to follow our star. Goals are dreams with a deadline.

Many of us have gone through a lifetime of taking chances. Most of us dreamed of being married and we promised to live with a mate whom we hardly knew, for better or for worse, when the decision meant "till death us do part." How foolhardy we were when we were young.

Then we dreamed of a family of our own and dashed headlong into producing children. What greater risk can one take than to create a new life? Fortunately, each child brings with him or her a place in the sun, and they grow up in spite of us.

Who in the Third Third has not imprudently changed jobs, brashly changed careers, courageously changed habitat, moving from relatives and long-term friends? Today is a new, no-limit day.

How fortunate we are to live in this era, in our country. With the easy life here, compared to that of many other people throughout the world, we can look forward to challenges in our golden years.

With the advances of modern medicine, our bodies can support what would have been impossible a few years ago.

Dreams can carry us soaring over the obstacles of reality. Fantasies that seem unattainable can become actuality. The barriers of the impossible dwindle by daring to dream boldly.

After I ran for state legislator in 1982 and lost, it seemed my days of dreaming were over. Advisers were quick to point out that, at 62, I should cool it. But it only hurts for a little while, and you tell yourself that there are other dreams.

The more forward we point ourselves, the further forward we go. Sure, sometimes we crash. Nobody achieves every goal. But the real achievement is to conquer the fear of trying.

Babe Ruth struck out more than 1,000 times but he had to step up to bat again and again to achieve the spectacular home run record for which we remember him.

When we're out there trying, all kinds of serendipitous things can happen. If we think positively, they're usually good things. Each person has a private illusion. One needs the imagination, the perspective and the stick-to-it-iveness.

Aging is not a factor. If anything, we're discovering at the end of the 20th Century that our capabilities increase as we cast off responsibilities that bogged us down in our youth. The accomplishments of people in their Third Third are legion. My friend Freddie, who had never held a racket until he retired, just won a tennis tournament at 69 after bypass surgery.

The older we get, the bolder we can get. We know that modesty can be a false value. What the heck—dare to dream.

Whoever thought in early 1985 that I would be a pen of antiquity, still writing columns. And who could ever fantasize that the creative stage producer Vinnette Carroll would write a play based on those columns? For me, it's a dazzling dream come true.

For me, and all of us, there will be more dreams tomorrow. It's not over yet.

The Young Live
Like There's No Tomorrow

◆

I saw a mother leaving the grocery store throw a candy wrapper on the street. Then her 6-year-old boy followed suit. It was at that point that I resigned as executive director of the world.

I've done my very best to keep things going properly for almost six decades, but it's getting out of hand, and I no longer want the responsibility.

If that anonymous woman in her 40s won't cooperate, then she and her offspring will have to live with things the way they create them. My last warning to my children's generation is, "Check your value system. Believe in what you're doing."

We in the Third Third have seen you through the biggest and best wars, the zillion-dollar space program, flowered toilet tissue, Disney World and deodorant spray. You'll have to take it from there.

For a while, I thought I could visit our wisdom upon a new generation eager to learn from history lest they repeat mistakes we have overcome. But the youngsters run things as if there were no tomorrow. Could they be right?

I ride along the super highways remembering politicians who promised us there would be landscaping and no billboards to mar the scenic views. What a crock! Surely the plethora of commercial signs add to the confusion, stress and accident rate. But if that's the way they want it, I'll learn to live with it.

If the current movers and shakers enjoy seeing blood and gore on the screen, both in the theater and on television, I won't be in the audience.

Would the beer and auto and soap merchants be spending millions of dollars if viewers were not responsive? Isn't the same medium sending the message that shooting, killing and violence is the way to go? Our children seem to be buying all of it.

Most in my generation have trouble understanding the new math and the system that says "buy now, pray later." Something's got to give in personal finances, or the fiscal structure of the federal government, if buying isn't curtailed when money is short. How do you figure those charge cards that charge you up to 18 percent for the privilege of owning something before you can afford it?

It must be the theory of "more is better" that creates the disposable society we can't get accustomed to. More sex and drugs, more computer games, more jobs in a career and more spouses in a lifetime seems to be today's measure of success.

"He who dies with the most toys, wins." The statistics about your "contentment quotient" don't read too well.

Can't you find some athletes or other heroes who don't indulge in steroids or other drugs?

Do you really want to pay these men millions of dollars to be role models for our youth? Give us back Jack Armstrong's example of the all-American boy. You say that was living in the past, and we say it doesn't have to be.

We're not in control any longer, but are you?

Do you really feel safer now that there's a gun in every home (and probably in most cars)? You've let the gun manufacturers sell you a bill of goods that is not good for our nation's safety. Now that you're well armed do you have to find a target to shoot? Please tell us there's a purpose in all this buildup of Star Wars for home and abroad. We'll not go out alone after dark (and you'd better not) for fear of those weapons.

All we do is pay our taxes; you're in the lead now.

Hard as we worked for the accumulation of our dollars, we had a defendable purpose in gathering money. Do you? Please tell us why you need to invest so much of yourselves in the pursuit of the dollar that you don't have time or interest or energy left for children, or for each other?

We'll vote for the lesser of evils that you present to us. We'll play golf and bridge and meet with each other to wonder where you're going: "Henny Penny, the sky is falling." We're worried for you and our grandchildren.

What is not changed for good in the world is generally not for lack of time or talent or energy. It is for the lack of will and the lack of courage. You are the most educated society the world has ever known, in the richest country. Let's see what you'll do with it.

On me, you shouldn't count to run the show anymore. But I could be available as a consultant.

Fruit Of Age
Is A Free Spirit

♦

I give warning to those around me about the power I feel in the Third Third. That power can lead to conduct devoid of concern about what my neighbor, or just about anyone else, thinks. Wise people use any empowerment to forward their purpose, but are careful not to injure others.

The Third Third gives us the power to enjoy. Each of us finds gratification in different ways and our choices of how to exercise the privilege of pleasure in these latter years differs from you to me.

I'm considering my alternatives. Perhaps I'll put aside work tomorrow and go bowling. I haven't run that weighty ball down the gutter for 20 years.

Maybe I'll visit the soon-to-be-built butterfly farm not far from where I live. I'd like to meet its developer. Can you imagine the creativity of someone who made that his occupation?

What would it be like to visit the children's ward at the local hospital? I could dress up in a funny mask and bring some dime store toys and books.

Perhaps skinny-dipping in the ocean on a chilly night would be a cool thing to do.

I think I'll phone my cousin Henry who dropped out of sight when his wife divorced him. I'll not let the fact that he owes me a call stand between us.

The inspiration for this "deviant" behavior comes from a poem by Britisher Jenny Joseph:

> When I am an old lady, I shall wear purple, with a red hat, which doesn't go and doesn't suit me.
>
> And I shall spend my pension on brandy and summer gloves, and satin sandals, and say we have no money for butter.
>
> I shall sit down on the pavement when I am tired and gobble up samples in shops and press alarm bells and run my stick along public railings and make up for the sobriety of my youth.
>
> I shall go out in my slippers in the rain and pick the flowers in other people's gardens and learn to spit . . . but maybe I ought to practice a little now, so people who know me are not too shocked and surprised when suddenly I am old and start to wear purple.

I already wear a lot of purple.

Buying and drinking brandy sounds pretty good to me, too. I'd want to be somewhat more purposeful in my aberrations. I'd want to live out some lifelong fantasies that I've not had the time or the gumption to do.

What would the world look like from a hot-air balloon that floats over the housetops?

Oh, to carry my new shoes while walking barefoot in a summer shower, and let my hair and clothes get soaking wet and not worry about catching cold because I'm not convinced that colds are contracted in that way and because from now on I'm willing to take my chances on the way I'll meet my end.

Or maybe I'll announce to my husband that I'm going to Russia even though he prefers to sit in front of his TV set. I'll send him a postcard.

I think I'll go wading in a canal, carefully, to feel the soft mushy slimy dirt between my toes. But I'll bring along a towel and a change of hose.

I'm going to get some clay and make a statue which I shall display in full view of the imaginary audience who will listen spellbound to my piano concert.

And on my birthday, I'll send a card to everyone I love to celebrate that I've reached another year in good health and good spirits and that I'm looking forward, forward.

Passion Is Revived
By A Well-Built Model

◆

I'm 68 years old this week, old enough to know better than to believe my husband when he says, "We'll buy any car you want, dear."

I have never developed an interest in cars. My motto is if it's clean and it runs, it's OK. I have a plethora of interests, but motor vehicles are not among them. An article I clipped and underlined stated as the cardinal rule in car buying: Don't fall in love with any one car. You'll lose your objectivity—and your negotiating edge.

Arnie, an otherwise dispassionate man, feels about cars. He is interested when the new models come out. He can debate with other men about the curves and lines of one over the other. He enjoys comparing. He observes the fine differences and innuendos between makes.

My husband is a quiet, soft-spoken, gentle man who can be believed on most occasions. He used to care a lot about "a slick chick" passing by, or "a good steak". But now, in the Third Third, when the sensual pleasures of life have long been available and he has tasted his fill of them, he doesn't express strong desires.

Thus, when he said that the choice of this car was completely mine, I believed. He suggested I start by looking at the Nissan Maxima.

Because I don't even know what I'm looking at or for, and want to be a wise consumer in spending this large a sum, I began my research.

Armed with various consumer's guides, we made our way to the showrooms.

We went to look at the Ford Taurus which was available in a flat (bench) seat. Low bucket seats in a small car are not comfortable for me, but, I was told by all the men around, "That's the beauty of the styling today." Our salesman seemed to think it relevant to tell me how agile his grandmother is in her 80's.

As the salesman pointed out the features, Arnie understood and felt and sensed, subliminally, what was being said. The very same car to him was attractive, seductive, tantalizing: a mean machine.

We tried other friend-recommended models. They were good cars, but for some illusive reason, lacked the personality to evoke masculine gusto, longing and desire.

No one asked me what I wanted in a car, nor did anyone wait for me to tell. All I want is a comfortable seat in a safe car that gets good mileage. Neither my personhood nor my image is vested in the shape of the car I drive. I'm not looking "to find myself" in sleek 4-color ads or in auto dealerships. I miss the relish of craving, the appetite, the thirst, the hunger for the illusion that a hyped machine can provoke.

The men, who in years past used to kick tires and slam doors to convince themselves this was the proper vehicle to buy, now have other means of emotional communication. They speak in tongues undiscernible to this "little old lady in tennis shoes."

Confused and exhausted, I begged for a stay of decision—time to study my literature for factors other than those the salesmen touted; pin stripes, wire hub caps, a moon-roof.

I cared about visibility, seat-belt comfort, climate control, door locks, mirrors and roominess. The manuals were not much help. They were not the Berlitz of man/car language.

They referred to such as a variable torque split with a rearward bias and naturally aspirated, turbocharged and intercooled engines. I don't know if I need to pay for leather wrapped steering wheel and shift handles or a rear defogger for a tropical climate. Do I want a spoiler?

I should have quit on the second trip out when Arnie suggested, "Let's look at the Maxima again." "Do you think it has changed?" I asked. "Never mind the sarcasm" he said, "I think you'll like it." I should have sensed by his tone of voice the signs of a man falling in love.

A week of shopping, studying, shifting led us to our self-imposed deadline for making a decision. My scope had narrowed down to a Taurus for the comfortable seat or the Acura for dependability. I was ready for D-Day. Arnie said, of course, I should buy whichever car I wanted. But before I make the final decision, just to look, with an open mind, at the Maxima.

With a turned-on, fervent, zealous gleam in his eye which I haven't seen in many years, Arnie signed the papers to order the Maxima.

I'll drive the other, older car. I love Arnie so I'll not deprive him of enjoying one of the last passions of his life.

Home Sweep Home

♦

There is talk about a new world in this generation; a world I can't conceive of. Rumor has it that there have been changes in what is defined as women's and men's work around the home. A recent study says that, with more than 60 percent of married women in the labor force, the men with whom they share their homes are sharing the household tasks. Great!

But I doubt it.

Not that I wouldn't be delighted if it were true. Not that I want to be a naysayer. Not that I don't want to see progress in my time. But there are some things that never change.

When it comes to household tasks, there is classic women's work and men's work. In our day, the routine grub work was relegated to the ladies. The heavier, occasional duties belonged to the man of the house.

The daily food planning, shopping and preparation, were the woman's purview, as were maintenance of clothing, washing, drying, folding, repairing.

Child care has definitely been mom's job: responsibility for physical, intellectual, educational, medical and religious well being. Fathers sometimes taught the kids to fish or play ball.

The household accounts and budgets were juggled by the Mrs., especially when more was needed than came in. In more affluent families, the man took charge of the money.

Socializing was the domain of women. Caring for elderly parents and maintaining relationships with relatives was also a feminine duty.

Men, in our generation, took on responsibility for the infrastructure of the house: electricity, plumbing, garbage disposal, heating and cooling. They also knew about and took care of cars.

As men began to talk about housework, they "helped out." The tasks were considered really women's work, but men gallantly, condescendingly and occasionally did the dishes or shopped.

A recent study based on research from the University of Maryland shows women are only doing 79 percent of meal preparation. Men are increasing their participation in bill paying to 34 percent; taking charge of 19 percent of the house cleaning. All this, we can presume, they do with a smile. This was not so in our time, and I find it difficult to believe.

The figures for men doing outdoor chores and repairs has not changed over the years, and remains at about 70 percent.

Guess I'm a die-hard, stuck in the past when men divested themselves of "Home Sweep Home."

My observation is that working women come home to the very same traditional women's tasks. Having it all can mean cleaning it all.

If the young husbands are, indeed, taking on some of the homemaking roles of their working wives, I want to witness that and congratulate them. I'll tip my hat to the man who cleans the inside of the shower curtain, takes over the wet (and worse) diapers, gets into the corners of the refrigerator, or washes the toilet bowl on a weekly basis.

I should live that long.

Love And Acceptance

◆

The drive back to Cincinnati was made more pleasant by having a new car with a tape deck. Anticipating a visit with our children and a party with old friends, we were on a joy ride, two old fools riding along to the air-conditioned hum that muted our singing along off-key, *What I'd Do for Love.*

It was a good trip. We had seen our children recently, so spending one day with them satisfied us for the time being.

Three days with a variety of friends were proof that, although the house and the neighborhood looked the same, our peers, also in their Third Third, had gone through changes. There was a contentedness on their faces that we see on old friends; the pleasure of being together again, finding each other well, working less and experiencing a general sense of well-being.

But attitudes have grown and changed over two decades. This is reality.

Sitting on the shaded porch with a drink brought us back

20 years to when we left. Then the children of "our crowd" were off to college and beyond. Now we review where they are and what they're doing.

After being dropped off by the child-care center van, Karl's 5-year-old granddaughter bounces in, thrusting at him a yo-yo she has made. He beams with appreciation. His 35-year-old daughter's biological clock was ticking too fast, so she decided to have this child without waiting for marriage. Karl, his wife and daughter, understand the difficulties. They are a nuclear family today.

With a shrug of the shoulders, Karl indicates his acceptance of reopening his home to an arrangement he would never have anticipated.

"Your ideas change," he says.

The eldest son of Jerry and Estelle is married to his third wife. The two first marriages brought three children. To stay in touch, the grandparents plan their annual vacations so they can visit them for short periods in distant cities. Their younger son's two former wives and children live nearby.

"You take life as it comes. We are present at each wedding," Jerry jokes, "but our wedding presents are not as large each time."

Ted and Annette tell us that next week they will be entertaining the parents of Marcy, their son's "live-in." To relieve my own discomfort, because I am a prude and uncomfortable with what I'm hearing, I offer, "This is today's dress rehearsal for marriage. Ha, ha."

No, I'm told, Marcy is still married to the father of her two children. When I unravel the threads of the story, I find my contemporaries aiding and abetting social situations that would have been unacceptable a generation ago. To people like me, it's hard to adapt to liberal moral codes.

It hurts to think of our children messing up their lives. Didn't the parents tell them that conformity is more comfortable? That conventionality is easier to live with? That breaking with mores, though exciting and romantic, can be dangerous and painful?

It's easier when the shoe is not pinching my foot. It's easier to make judgments in the abstract.

"You'd go along," says Ted. "Kids don't ask what to do with their lives. It's either you accept their choice of lifestyle or you create a rift and lose them."

The role of parenting has altered over the years. Once we were there to point the way and tell the kids they would be responsible for their actions. Now we help pick up the pieces if things go wrong.

We remember the errant actions of our own children that we took as a personal afront, until we eased into receptivity. We gave them life, and it's theirs to live.

On the ride home, we listened more thoughtfully to the taped words: *We did what we had to do. Can't forget, can't regret what we did for love.*

We've Earned Our Aches, Pains and Foibles

◆

I t's all in the way you look at it. Your life is either half full or half empty.

There's sarcastic writing in newspapers and magazines about ways to tell whether you're over the hill. They don't bring a smile to my lips, let alone a belly laugh. Since I'm one of those over-the-hill folks, let me put in a few words of my own.

"You get winded playing chess."

At least we're participating in a sport, not just spectating.

"You look forward to a dull evening."

Sure we do. We've been around the block a few times and don't have to go chasing for thrills.

"Your knees buckle and your belt won't."

Gravity has been pulling at this bod for almost seven decades. What's your excuse?

"You burn the midnight oil until 9:30 p.m."

We've learned that early to bed and early to rise brings health, wealth and wisdom. Who wouldn't want to accumulate those things? Besides, we've found mornings to be as bright and exciting as dark nights.

"Everything hurts, and what doesn't hurt doesn't work."

The younger generation taught us: "No pain, no gain."

"Your little black book contains only names ending in M.D."

Doctors have to make a living. Yes, we're becoming accustomed to supporting their life style.

"The gleam in your eye is from the sun hitting your bifocals."

Look again, young'un. The gleam in our eye is from all the pleasant memories.

"Your favorite part of the newspaper is '25 Years Ago Today.'"

Now that you mention it, things then were better in many ways. The good guys had a better chance of winning then.

"You turn out the lights for reasons of economy, not romantic reasons."

Don't kid yourselves, kids. Our romance doesn't depend on environment; we don't need a thing but the right person. Our generation found lovers and pretty much was satisfied. The romantic track record of your generation doesn't seem to be so great.

"Your pacemaker makes the garage door go up when an attractive member of the opposite sex walks by."

Well, we're still alive, ain't we?

"You can't operate the TV without the remote control." And, "You regularly use the word 'newfangled'."

What's the big deal? We've operated during much more complex situations, like gearing up for war, milking a cow and cranking a car. Newfangled electronic devices are a piece of cake for us.

"You are offended by the things they say on radio these days." And, "Easy-listening radio doesn't sound as bland as it used to."

Darn right we're offended by 2 Live Crew and the likes!

And much of what's on TV, on stage, in concerts, in art, in books. But we'll defend to the death your right to that freedom.

"You could talk for at least 15 minutes on the subject of gum disease."

We can, and we do. Charge that up to the cost of a long and tasty life. Nothing could have prevented that. What about your AIDS, herpes or overdosing, which you, sadly, bring on yourselves?

"You don't like it when someone sits in 'your chair'."

My chair? Now you're getting serious.

Listen, kiddo, you should have such memories. I wish the same for you baby boomers and yuppies in your own Third Third years.

We know we're comfortably old when we can relax and stop swimming upstream. We dealt with harder times than you've known. We changed what we could and accepted what we couldn't.

What will you accomplish in your lifetime?

Ha, ha. She who laughs last laughs best.